An American Community Celebrates the Bicentennial of the United States Constitution: Essays and Presentations

Edited by Joseph A. Losco
and Thomas A. Sargent

BALL STATE UNIVERSITY   Muncie, Indiana

© Ball State University 1988

ISBN 0-937994-11-1

Library of Congress Catalog Card No. 88-63563

88512 up

Contents

Introduction

In 1987, all the states and hundreds of communities across this country held celebrations to commemorate the bicentennial of the American Constitution. In the states that were formed out of the Old Northwest Territory, appropriate celebrations also noted the bicentennial of the Northwest Ordinance of 1787.

The bicentennial observances are continuing as we record the ratification of the Constitution, the beginnings of the Congress and the presidency under the new governance document, and the addition of the Bill of Rights.

Ball State University and the Muncie community shared in celebrating the bicentennial by organizing a series of events designed to call attention to the anniversary, to provide background on the events of 1787 and beyond, and to encourage reflection on the contemporary role of the Constitution in our daily lives. (A complete schedule of the activities and a list of the members of the Community-University Advisory Committee appear at the end of this book.)

We began with a series of lectures and presentations on the world of 1787 in which local scholars discussed the political events, the literature, the architecture, and the arts of the time. A dramatic presentation brought into sharp focus the conflicts of the Constitutional Convention in the summer of 1787. A series of three town meetings brought to the community experts on various current constitutional issues to discuss those problems with local participants. The Muncie Symphony Orchestra focused on a history of American music during its summer open-air concert, and later in the summer the Special Collections division of Bracken Library mounted an exhibition of rare documents dealing with the Constitution and the Northwest Ordinance. The materials were lent to Ball State by the Lilly Library at Indiana University, Bloomington. A special event was the costumed impression of James Madison given by Dr. James Soles, professor of political science at the University of Delaware. The concluding events in the schedule were lectures by two of America's

1

most distinguished historians, Richard Morris of Columbia University and Michael Kammen of Cornell University.

Selections from the events have been included in this book. The world of 1787 is represented by essays by Andrew Cayton and Robert Habich. Dr. Cayton suggests that the most important heritage from the eighteenth-century Constitution may be the vision of the men who wrote it and the process by which it was created, rather than the document itself. Dr. Habich puts forth the idea that the literature of the early federal period reflected its time and the needs of Americans in that period, a time far different from our own.

The script of the dramatic presentation on the formation of the Constitution clearly reveals the great conflicts and personal anguish of many of the delegates who wrestled during a hot summer with the issues presented by writing a governance document. The script is designed to be read by the actors, and the emphasis is on the words and thoughts rather than the action.

No celebration of the legacy of the U.S. Constitution would be complete without paying tribute to the way in which the document continues to frame current debate. That debate is expressed in the presentations from three town meetings organized around constitutionally based issues that have generated considerable discussion in the last few years and that are likely to remain important concerns for the rest of this century. The meetings were intended not only to serve as a forum for the exploration of difficult philosophical, legal, and political issues, but also to underline the continued relevance of the Constitution to twentieth-century issues and controversies. Each meeting featured two distinguished spokespersons offering different points of view. The presentations generated debate that was often lively and extended, a feature that the founders would no doubt have appreciated.

The subject of the first meeting was pornography and the First Amendment. Leading the discussion of these issues were Marcia Pally, a free-lance writer and artist, and J. Michael Loomis, a deputy county prosecutor.

The second meeting featured a discussion of school prayer. Although the issue was temporarily laid to rest in *Engle* v. *Vitale* and *Abington* v. *Schempp*, the constitutionality of prayer in public schools has resurfaced with renewed fervor, and two nationally recognized scholars were invited to address the question. Dean M. Kelley is head of the National Council of Churches and Dr. James Hitchcock is a professor of history at St. Louis University.

The third meeting addressed the thorny issue of interpreting the Constitution itself. Morton Frisch and Frederick Schauer were the featured guests for that discussion. Frisch is a professor of political science at Northern Illinois University, and Schauer is a professor of law at the University of Michigan Law School.

The final selection from the celebration events is the essay by Richard Morris containing his observations on the Constitution, stressing again the process by which the document was written, the compromises reached, and the flexibility it contained.

Funding for the university-community observance of the bicentennial was provided by Ball State University and grants from the Indiana Committee for the Humanities, the Ball Brothers Foundation, and United Ministries at Ball State.

This publication is designed to be a permanent record of the events by which we celebrated the bicentennial and to allow further reflection by all of us on the events, the persons, the times, and, most of all, the ideas involved in writing the United States Constitution.

Joseph A. Losco
Associate Professor of Political Science

Thomas A. Sargent
Professor of Political Science
Director, E. B. and Bertha C. Ball Center
    for University and Community Programs

July 1988

The Constitution and the Northwest Ordinance: Governing a New Nation

Andrew R. L. Cayton

The Constitution of the United States, wrote the British prime minister William Gladstone in the late nineteenth century, was "the most wonderful work ever struck off at a given time by the brain and purpose of man." Few Americans, past or present, would quarrel with Gladstone's judgment. Indeed, one of the most remarkable things about the document that created the basic structure of our government is how quickly and how thoroughly it became the object of almost mystical reverence. Today, most Americans approach the original parchment, sealed in a glass case in the National Archives, as if they were visiting a religious shrine. Though it has always been subject to amendment and interpretation, the Constitution exudes an aura and a power that approach, if they do not exceed, those of scripture.

The celebration of the two-hundredth birthday of the Constitution would thus be a major event in American society as a matter of course. But the significance of the anniversary is heightened by the fact that we live in an era of especially strong worship of the Constitution. In the 1980s, candidates for political office inform us that the document was divinely inspired, while the attorney general of the United States insists that judicial interpretations of the Constitution conform to the intentions of its authors. And President Ronald Reagan constantly invokes the rhetoric and spirit of the Founding Fathers as justification for his policies, both foreign and domestic.

The enthusiasm of a renewed respect for the Constitution is also part of the current crusade for a return to basics in American public education. William Bennett, the secretary of education, worries that "the principles of the Founders, the traditions embodied in our institutions, the memories of our forefathers' sacrifices, the examples of our statesmen" may not "be alive in the next generation's minds and hearts." Throughout American history, Bennett believes, "certain ideals and aspirations" run "like a golden thread."

4

What are they? Well, we the people, all of us, believe in liberty, and equality. We believe in limited government and in the betterment of the human condition. These truths underlie both our history and our society; they define us as a people; and while they may be self-evident, they are not spontaneously apprehended by the young.

Whether one agrees or disagrees with the secretary's definition of the "truths" of American history, his comments succinctly illustrate the point that many Americans—or at least those in positions of power—believe that the Constitution of the United States is a vital and basic part of the world of 1986–87.

Historians of the American Revolution tend to view pronouncements such as Bennett's—as well as the general public display of affection for the Constitution that surrounds its bicentennial—with ambivalence. On the one hand, they delight in the attention paid to the people and events they study every day, and they glory in the opportunities made available to discuss the details and significance of the past. Who does not enjoy being an authority, particularly if it brings some small degree of fame and fortune? On the other hand, historians cringe at the superficiality and ephemeral qualities of public celebrations of the past. One of the most important responsibilities of historians in any society is to preserve the sanctity of the past, to protect the lives and words of our predecessors from misappropriation and misuse in the present. So, in a strange way, historians are like fish out of water at a bicentennial event: they are interested in keeping inviolate the distinctiveness, the separateness of the past. Most Americans, on the other hand, from the president on down, want to celebrate universal truths, or what we have in common with our ancestors (meaning of course, what *we*, not *they*, think is important about them).

The 1986 celebration of the centennial of the Statue of Liberty is a good example of this tension. Historians wanted to talk about historical context, about the difficulties, tensions, and unique experiences of the immigration process; most people wanted to hear about such general ideas as democratic aspirations and American freedom. Scholarly wisdom was hardly ignored, but it was definitely not part of the main event. What professional historian, of whatever political persuasion, failed to empathize with President Reagan as he stood on the deck of the USS *John F. Kennedy* on the evening of July 4 talking about Thomas Jefferson and John Adams while millions of Americans were impatiently waiting to see fireworks?

Fortunately, since this essay is not being followed by any kind of pyrotechnical display, it presents an opportunity to talk about the historical context in which the Constitution was written, about the distinctiveness, the complexity, the tensions and problems of the

United States in 1787. The essay proceeds, however, from the firm conviction that a historical perspective on that era is part of a larger argument about the nature and future of American society in the 1980s. The historian's professional concern with the sanctity of the past does not exclude him or her from participation in the debates of the present. If it did, there would be no reason, beyond the pleasure of antiquarianism, for historians to exist.

My major contention is simple. The Constitution of the United States was the product of the efforts of a tiny group of white males, operating under assumptions about human nature and society peculiar to the eighteenth century, to bring their definition of order to the aspirations and difficulties of the wide variety of peoples who inhabited thirteen loosely connected former colonies on the far frontier fringes of European civilization. Historians are trained to see the Constitution as an eighteenth-century document written by eighteenth-century men to deal with eighteenth-century concerns. On the surface, viewing the Constitution in this way may seem of little importance to residents of one of the most powerful nations on this planet at the end of the twentieth century. But what ultimately matters about the world of 1787, the universal connection between past and present that overrides professional obsession with the distinctiveness of the past, is not the Constitution and the intentions of its authors. Rather, it is the spirit of experimentation and human creation, the sense of possibility, potential, and change, that permeated that era.

As a historian I am appalled by the notion that we should govern ourselves by ways of thinking and acting that are two hundred years old. As important as it is to revere and conserve the past, it is just as important, on occasion, to break with history and to embrace new worlds as well. In other words, perhaps the great legacy of the Founding Fathers for us is not the ways in which they stayed true to the past but the ways in which they used the past to imagine the future.

It is too easy to forget in the midst of bicentennial self-congratulation that the Constitution of 1787 was a very controversial document in its time. The members of the Philadelphia Convention signed the document in September 1787. It took a year for individual state conventions to approve it. George Washington, after all, did not assume office as the first president of the United States until early 1789. The debates in the state conventions were long and tough; many prominent Americans, among them Patrick Henry and Samuel Adams, opposed the Constitution. North Carolina and Rhode Island did not approve the Constitution at first and in several other states (notably Massachusetts, Virginia, and New York) a handful of votes made all the difference. The Constitution was never put to a direct popular vote, but there is good reason to believe that if it had been, it would not have been approved.

Why not? Why did many Americans in 1787 not see what William Gladstone saw and what William Bennett in 1986 clearly sees? The answer, to a great extent, lies in the localistic and pluralistic nature of American society in the 1780s. The Constitution of 1787 was a political outline of a very specific vision of the American future and a very specific definition of what it meant to be an American. And the men who wrote it, whom we call Federalists, represented only one part of the pluralistic world of 1787. Many other Americans found the Federalists' ideas dangerous; indeed, many believed they undid the American Revolution.

The world of 1787 consisted of several separate but interlocking worlds. The United States at the end of the eighteenth century was a fragile entity with a brief history and uncertain prospects. More often than not, people identified themselves as residents of a state or region, as Virginians or Pennsylvanians. To be sure, they were all Americans. But what exactly did that mean?

Americans in the eighteenth century lacked the confidence of William Bennett in answering that question. So do historians. In fact, it is easier to say what being an American was not, which may be the crucial point. The United States in 1787 was as pluralistic and as diverse as the United States in 1987, perhaps more so.

The population of the decade-old republic was approximately four million people who did not share a common ethnic or cultural background. Twenty percent were African, 9 percent were German, 10 to 15 percent were Scots-Irish, and significant numbers were Dutch, French, and Spanish. Even the large number of English people varied in customs and attitudes, depending on the part of the country from which their ancestors had migrated.

The United States was a collection of locally oriented societies, cultures defined by differences in economic and ideological structures. Most people were farmers; urban residents made up slightly more than 5 percent of the population (although they exercised disproportionate economic and political power). But work habits and social customs varied widely from region to region. Semi-subsistence agriculture practiced in the corners of New England was not the same as the plantation agriculture of Tidewater Virginia or the cereal-producing farms of southeastern Pennsylvania.

Americans were also divided by wealth. By European standards, differences in standards of living among Americans do not seem so great. The homes of a Virginia aristocrat like George Washington or a Boston merchant prince like John Hancock pale in contrast to the palatial estates and opulent life-styles of the English and French nobilities. As a whole Americans ate better, dressed better, were in better health, and lived longer than their European counterparts. If you were unlucky enough to be poor in 1787, you would have been far better off in Boston or Philadelphia than anywhere else in the world.

But the fact that American society was comparatively egalitarian should not blind us to the fact that inequalities did exist. The work of several recent historians clearly shows the gap between rich and poor widening in eighteenth-century America. Wealth was increasingly concentrated in fewer and fewer hands and, as a whole, the American standard of living frequently declined in the 1700s. Poverty was a problem in American cities, and farmers in New England found themselves living in what one historian has called "a world of scarcity." Most obvious in retrospect, of course, is the fact that the 20 percent of Americans who were black not only did not own property; they were considered to be property themselves.

Religious practices also divided Americans in 1787. Here again, on a superficial level, the people had much in common. The fact is that they were overwhelmingly Protestant. But within that general rubric existed a bewildering array of denominations, ranging from Anglicanism to Congregationalism to Dutch Reformed to evangelical sects such as the Baptists and the Methodists. From the so-called Great Awakening of the 1730s and 1740s, American religions had been dividing and redividing like the cells of the human body. In short, while almost all Americans worshipped the same God, they understood Him and paid respect to Him in any number of different ways.

Also growing in importance in the aftermath of the revolution were divisions based on gender and race. The War for Independence and the rhetoric of democratic equality had touched all Americans. Many women and blacks asserted themselves in the 1780s and 1790s in ways they would never have contemplated fifty years earlier. When Abigail Adams playfully told her husband John to "remember the ladies" or when the black physician Benjamin Banneker wrote to Secretary of State Thomas Jefferson about the intellectual capabilities of Afro-Americans, they were forcefully pointing out that the world of 1787 was not the exclusive province of white males.

Cutting across these cultural and economic differences were sectional rivalries and state jealousies. Virginians tended to find New Englanders cold and pious, while New Englanders distrusted the effusiveness and passion of Southerners. In political terms, states were strong guardians of their rights and privileges. In the 1770s, members of Congress had written the Articles of Confederation—the outline of the structure of government superseded by the Constitution of 1787—with the intention of protecting state sovereignty. In the same spirit, such leading American statesmen as Patrick Henry, Thomas Jefferson, Samuel Adams, John Hancock, and George Clinton preferred to exercise power on the state level in the decade after 1775 and to leave service in the national Congress to younger, less experienced men.

Fundamentally, then, there was no such thing as a typical American in 1787. Reinforcing and confirming the localistic and pluralistic quality of life in the United States were the incredible difficulties of transportation and communication. Mail delivery was irregular at best, and roads were miserable if they existed at all. The best as well as the cheapest means of travel and conveyance was water. This situation was fine for people along the Atlantic Coast and such navigable rivers as the Connecticut, the Hudson, the Delaware, and the Potomac. But it was of no use to people who lived only a few miles from water. This was a world in which news travelled from Rome to London no faster than it had in the days of Julius Caesar. Americans in the cities along the coast had more contact with Europe than they did with the interior for the simple reason that it was easier to get goods and information from Philadelphia to London than it was to get them from Philadelphia to Pittsburgh.

Indeed, arguably the most important division in the American society of 1787 was between those who lived near navigable water and those who did not. The residents of cities and the Tidewater South, economic and religious differences notwithstanding, were tied into a growing world of international commerce. The eighteenth century was a time of tremendous expansion for capitalistic economies based on the rules of supply and demand, the pursuit of individual profit, and the power of the market. Cultural and political exchange, moreover, accompanied economic exchange. Thus the residents of Boston, Philadelphia, Charleston, and the river plantations of Virginia found themselves involved in the world of western Europe; they bought goods in Europe, they looked to Europe for books, fashions, and ideas. They had more in common with Europeans than they did with Americans who lived away from cities and rivers.

The latter group nonetheless constituted the majority of the new nation's citizens. They were hardly ignorant barbarians. But they did live in relatively isolated communities and their contacts (economic and cultural) with the wider world were fleeting. Their concern was with the survival of family and the protection of local traditions. They were not as interested in making money or improving the human condition as were the residents of areas with easy access to navigable rivers or the Atlantic Ocean. On the contrary, they tended to be suspicious of change and innovation, which threatened the continuity and predictability of their lives. And, not surprisingly, many of them were opposed to the adoption of the Constitution.

By and large, the Federalists and their supporters were well-educated residents of the more commercially developed parts of the United States. They were also generally men with a great deal of national experience. Many of them were former army officers and members of Congress. Above all, they were men whose lives had been lived beyond the local level, men who were much more intimately involved than the average American in the expanding economic and cultural world of the international marketplace.

Thus, the Federalists were very much concerned with the young republic's standing in the world. They worried that the government of the United States—which lacked, along with the power to tax, effective military and diplomatic establishments under the Articles of Confederation—was not being taken seriously by other nations. If Americans intended to engage in stable and prosperous trade with the rest of the world, the Federalists believed that they would have to convince the rest of the world that they had a government capable of asserting and protecting their interests. In the same vein, they contended that a respected member of the international community would have a unified, coordinated economic policy and a central judicial system. In simple terms, the Federalists hoped that the Constitution would do what the Articles of Confederation could not do—create a strong national government with the power to develop and enforce a national consensus by overriding the multiplicity of state whims and local customs. It was this goal that led James Madison to think of a national veto over the actions of state legislatures as crucial to the success of the whole document.

But the Federalists had much more in mind than merely strengthening the power of the government of the United States by giving it the authority to tax and to regulate commerce. They had cultural and social concerns as well. Indeed, they envisioned the Constitution as a means of reforming and readjusting the basic structures of American society. As men of national experience and international perspective, the Federalists shared what might be labelled a cosmopolitan outlook on the world. And most of them were appalled by the vulgar aspects of American society in the 1780s—the parochialism, the provincialism, the heated defenses of local prerogatives, and bald assertions of individual rights.

What the Federalists wanted was to make the United States the climax of the economic, social, and cultural development of European civilization. The achievement of these ends, however, as men such as Alexander Hamilton well knew, depended on the destruction of the pervasive localism of American life. If the United States was to become what the Federalists intended it to become—the strongest, most prosperous, most culturally advanced nation in history, the rival of Augustan Rome and eighteenth-century Britain, it would have to become a united country in economic, social, and cultural as well as political ways.

Most cosmopolitan Americans assumed that all societies passed through predictable stages of social and economic development. The history of the Western world, they believed, was a cycle of individual progressions from barbarism to civilization followed sadly but inevitably by rapid declines back to the depths of barbarism as people became selfish and indolent. The tragic histories of Greece and Rome exemplified this pattern. In the first stages, men and women lived in isolation, their lives geared to subsistence economies; they had little interest, as a result, in education or refinement. At the other extreme, in societies at the highest stages of economic development, people lived in a world of interdependence. International commerce and economic specialization marked their lives; they devoted increasing amounts of time to polishing and ornamenting themselves and their world. In the former kind of society, people dealt with each other in the most primitive ways imaginable: local prejudices stood in the way of harmony and fomented conflicts and contention. In the latter world, the peaceful exchange of both goods and ideas and the existence of powerful institutions such as schools, churches, and strong central governments paved the path to harmony, balance, and order.

In general, the Federalists hoped to create a national government in 1787 that would lay the foundations of a great commercial empire— a nation unencumbered by parochial jealousies and state rivalries, a nation governed by laws and the requirements of the international marketplace of goods and ideas. The Federalists thought of the future of the United States in continental terms. The concept of empire did not necessarily encompass colonial expansion, but it did involve the nation on a grand scale. America had the resources and the opportunity to mold itself into a dominant economic and political power. To fail to develop the young republic into a model of the highest levels of economic and cultural achievements would be to betray their responsibility to both the living and future generations.

To achieve this goal, the Federalists turned to history. The members of the Philadelphia convention were familiar with the outlines of the past, especially the histories of Greece, Rome, and all attempts at republican government. The particular model many Federalists had in mind was Great Britain. Between 1660 and 1760 that nation had risen from a position of weakness and confusion to one of international dominance. An island country wracked by internal conflicts in the 1650s, Britain in the 1750s had emerged as the most powerful nation on the earth. The critical period in this transformation in the eyes of eighteenth-century Americans was the years between 1688 and 1720. In those decades, the British had achieved political stability, established the basic institutions of their economic power, resolved long-standing religious and dynastic issues, and laid the foundations of their military and naval power. Britain's worldwide trade made London the center of international business. And victories in a succession of wars with France made the English the foremost power in Europe. With increasing economic and political might came an outpouring of literary and artistic achievement. England between 1660 and 1760 had encouraged such scientists as Isaac Newton; had produced such writers as Pope, Swift, Defoe, Gay, Addison, Steele, and Fielding; had nurtured musicians like Purcell and Handel; and had fostered the work of such artists as Gainsborough, Reynolds, and Hogarth. Above all, it had given the world statesmen on the order of Marlborough, Godolphin, Walpole, Bolingbroke, and Pitt. To American Federalists in the late eighteenth century, Britain in the early 1700s was one of those rare times (the Augustan age of Rome was another) when men had been able to fashion a society that enriched and improved mankind. (Never mind that England's development had also created incredible poverty and social disorder and destroyed much of traditional life.)

The Federalists who met in Philadelphia in 1787 hoped that the proposed constitution would be the beginning of a similar transformation in the United States. To be sure, they did not want to turn America into an imitation Britain; they recognized the impact of the American Revolution and were committed to some form of republican government. An American empire would be an improved version of early eighteenth-century Britain; just as powerful, just as prosperous, just as advanced, but also more democratic and less corrupt. The Federalists, in short, intended to foster economic development, political stability, and cultural creativity in order to fashion the United States into the most glorious society the world had ever known.

But they also recognized the fact that the divided and localistic nature of American society in the 1780s was a major obstacle to their ends. Alexander Hamilton, George Washington, and James Madison did not need historians to tell them that the United States was a compendium of peoples of different economic, political, ethnic, and religious backgrounds. The great danger in the eyes of the Federalists was that ordinary Americans' petty personal and local concerns would destroy the glorious future of a republican empire. To many members of the gentry in the 1780s, the universal American defense of local interests had become a sign of stagnation or social decay. Americans had gotten too much in the habit in the 1760s and 1770s of rising in righteous indignation and rebellion against every imagined threat against their freedoms. The latest case in point was Shay's Rebellion, the uprising in Massachusetts of farmers angry about high taxes and an unresponsive legislature, which had been suppressed by state troops in the winter of 1787.

The Constitution laid the foundations for the Federalists' efforts to overcome pervasive American localism and pluralism. It created a strong national government, a powerful central, overarching authority, which would replace local parochialism with national purpose. The Federalists were committed to what Cathy Matson and Peter S. Onuf, two recent historians, have called a form of neo-mercantilism. They believed that "enterprise could cement the union and redeem nature's promise of boundless prosperity *if* interests were properly protected, promoted, and harmonized. 'Independence' implied an interdependence of interests throughout the union as well as national 'respectability' and power at home and abroad." Only an activist national government could achieve these goals.

The Constitution was an embodiment of popular sovereignty, but it outlined a system for filtering decision making through several stages in an effort to counteract local and special interests. The election of the president by the electoral college, the choice of senators by state legislatures, the length of terms, and the staggering of senatorial elections, the creation of a national judiciary chosen for life by the Senate and president—were all intended to vitiate popular control over the national government. In the Federalist scheme of things, only a supreme national authority, unquestioned and uncompromised, could overcome American localism and lead the new republic to its imperial destiny.

Of course, the problem here is that this was the perspective of only a small group of men. Other people—many of them residents of less-developed regions of the United States—saw what they were proposing quite simply as a repudiation of the American Revolution.

The Constitution, its critics believed, created a strong national government with the power to tax and to destroy local privileges and traditions, a development, they were quick to point out, that they and their parents had gone to war in the 1770s to stop. Indeed, such men as Patrick Henry asked, was it not the desire to escape the interference of central authority in their affairs that had led them to revolution in the first place?

The Federalists, of course, replied that the new American government, unlike the old British one, rested on the explicit consent of the governed. For them popular sovereignty—embodied in the three words "we the people"—made all the difference in the world. The Federalists were right. But so were their critics. True, the new federal government rested on popular consent. But the Constitution did create a political structure that directly challenged the preeminence of local rights and sovereignty in American society.

The Federalist vision was a noble one, which is precisely what made it so offensive to many contemporary Americans even as it seems so appealing to us. Men like Washington and Hamilton had a heroic approach to life. They were less interested in personal fortune and popular adulation than they were in fame, the immortality of their public reputation. Twice in his life, George Washington surrendered power voluntarily, thereby exchanging enhanced contemporary influence for enhanced historical eminence. Alexander Hamilton achieved positions of power through patronage, not elections. Their ultimate goal was to achieve immortality by creating a powerful government that would bring order and homogeneity to the United States. In the Federalist vision of the future, to be an American citizen would mean to be the model for the civilized world.

In the 1790s, the administrations of Washington and John Adams would try to make this dream a reality by laying national economic foundations in the forms of the national debt, national bank, and national taxes; by laying national political foundations in the forms of a strong military, impressive display of presidential formality, and attacks on state privileges; and by laying national cultural foundations in the forms of awful heroic prose and poetry, symbols of American homogeneity, and the construction of a miniature Rome on a God-forsaken swamp on the Potomac River.

In so doing, of course, the Federalists were sailing against the wind, for their vision was at odds with the facts that American society was parochial and pluralistic and that the major legacy of the revolution for most Americans was the apotheosis of local rights. In fact, the glue that held the United States together throughout most of the nineteenth century was nothing more than a tacit acceptance of diversity. Periodic efforts to enforce homogeneity aside, what defined the United States as a whole was pluralism, a fact that became more apparent with the industrial development of the country and the massive immigration of Europeans and Asians of a wide variety of religious and cultural backgrounds. Various groups attempted to create cultural norms on the local or state levels, but the dominant motif of nineteenth-century American politics on the national level was laissez-faire. The weakness of the federal government was less a result of ideological commitment, however, than of the simple fact that homogeneity was usually unenforceable. Americans were not willing to fight a bloody civil war over every issue. In an ironic way, America became an empire in the twentieth century in spite of itself.

When we are thinking carefully, I think that few of us today would wish to be governed by the principles and assumptions of the Federalists. To do so would be to embrace a world in which blacks were slaves, women were treated as nonentities, and the dominant characteristic of the nation's leaders was an utter lack of respect for the intelligence and culture of the mass of American citizens; it would be to subject ourselves to political structures and ideas developed for a largely agricultural, sparsely settled outpost of civilization. Just as important, to do so would be to ignore two hundred years of American history. The history of the United States has not been a gradual working out of the vision of the Founding Fathers. To the contrary, the history of the United States has involved putting the principles and spirit of men such as Washington, Jefferson, and Hamilton to use in the present. The world of 1987 and the world of 1787 are not the same, and we should not expect to govern ourselves in the same ways. The men who wrote the Constitution could not have conceived of the kind of world in which we live; more to the point, we have a difficult time conceiving of their world.

I do not want to conclude this essay by leaving the impression that history is unimportant. Obviously, I do not believe that. But I do think we can study history more profitably if we concentrate less on the enshrinement of the specific, tangible achievements of our ancestors—the Constitution, for example—and focus our attention on their methods, their assumptions, and their processes. When the Federalists set out to create a new government for the United States, they turned first and foremost to history for guidance; they looked to Rome, they looked to England. But when they wrote the Constitution they used the lessons of history to make something new, something that drew on the unique past to deal with the unique present. If Americans learn anything from the celebration of the bicentennial of the Constitution, if we remember anything about our Founding Fathers, I hope it is their effort to create their vision of the future, however utopian. To worship an eighteenth-century document at the end of the twentieth century as the pinnacle of political thought and organization is, in many ways, to betray the spirit and the trust of the men who wrote it.

Writing the Wrongs: American Literature in Defense of the New Nation

Robert D. Habich

Was there American literature in the 1780s? Feel no embarrassment if you cannot immediately think of any titles; part of my purpose is to suggest some good reasons why people of discernment and taste often cannot. And partly, too, I want to explore with you the ways in which our earliest national literature was part of the larger drive for self-definition that characterized our cultural and political life during the period of the constitutional debate.

In my undergraduate classes I refer to the early national period—roughly 1776 to 1800—as the Baby Huey phase of American literature. The label may make other historians gag, but we literary historians tend to be more tolerant of such things. Baby Huey, you may recall, was the enormous prepubescent duck of comic book fame, good-natured, well-meaning, not yet out of diapers but endowed with a body and strength out of proportion to its mind. Like Baby Huey, the American literary community at this time struggled to gain control over its own vast potential; as with Baby Huey, we are apt to remember its sometimes comic lack of coordination rather than its earnestness and its strengths. Perhaps a more fitting tag for the age was the one it gave itself countless times, from the title of a Philip Freneau poem of 1775. This was the time of the "rising glory of America." Fully as well as its lawmakers and its statesmen, America's writers were conscious of that rising glory and, as my title suggests, defensive about it. In their various ways, and with decidedly varied degrees of artistic success, they tried to create a body of literature worthy of the new nation, one that would both justify and help to define the character of the infant United States.

What was it like to be a writer in those years? We might well look first at what it was like to be a reader. In the 1780s higher education remained largely confined to the upper classes, but in the original colonies, at least, there was widespread literacy; farmers, artisans, laborers—a remarkable portion of them could read and write, almost 90 percent of white adults by the early nineteenth century, according to some estimates (Nye 250). The wealthy amassed personal libraries of thousands of volumes, and even people of lesser means owned books. We know this from wills and other records of estates, where books often figured prominently among the items bequeathed to heirs. Simple ownership of books, of course, does not guarantee that people read them. But there is other evidence of the appetite of the American reading public—the increasing number of bookstores, for instance, or the rise of private subscription libraries, where for a membership fee one could borrow the latest books. By the time of the American Revolution, Boston had about fifty bookstores, Philadelphia more than thirty (Nye 250). Similarly, the period just after the revolution saw a tremendous rise in the number of newspapers, probably the most accurate measure of popular literacy. By conservative estimates there were 150 dailies and weeklies by the turn of the century, a number that would double by 1810 and continue to double again each decade through 1830 (Hart 67; Nye 251). A traveller in the American East observed in 1772, probably with only small exaggeration, "Such is the prevailing taste for books of every kind, that almost every man is a reader." Some twenty years later a visitor from London made the same startled observation: "If John goes to town with a load of hay, he is charged to be sure not to forget to bring home 'Peregrine Pickle's Adventures,' and when Dolly is sent to market to sell her eggs, she is commissioned to purchase 'The History of Pamela Andrews.' In short all ranks and degrees now READ" (Hart 39, 53).

What else were John and Dolly reading in the 1780s? If we keep in mind that in the eighteenth century—indeed, in the next one too—the definition of literature included writing about history, politics, religion, and science, as well as imaginative art such as poetry, fiction, and drama, we will recognize that the preferences of the American reading public were as diverse as the readers themselves. Bestsellers published in American editions in the 1770s include Oliver Goldsmith's *The Vicar of Wakefield*, Laurence Sterne's *Tristram Shandy*, Defoe's *Robinson Crusoe*, Milton's *Paradise Lost*, James Thomson's *The Seasons*, and Lord Chesterfield's *Letters to His Son* (Mott, *Golden Multitudes* 304)—all but the last of these among the acknowledged classics of English literature. The 1780s saw the popularity of Samuel Richardson's novel *Clarissa*, William Cowper's poem about country life, *The Task*, and Robert Burns's collected *Poems*. Add to these such best-selling works of history and politics as Gibbon's *Decline and Fall of the Roman Empire*, the *Federalist Papers*, and a religious work like Richard Watson's *Apology for the Bible*, and you have some idea of the range and maturity of American literary tastes at the time (Hart 303).

To narrow our inquiry further, imaginative literature—fiction, poetry, and drama—enjoyed a warm reception in the American 1780s. The novel, probably the most important literary genre of the century, was as popular here as in England. To be sure, there was still widespread suspicion of novels; they were, critics charged, not true, therefore lies, therefore time-wasters that softened the mind and polluted the imagination. The title of an often reprinted article in the popular press pinpoints some of the anxiety: "Novel Reading a Cause of Female Depravity." (Males, we assume, found other causes.) But the warnings of stern moralists did little to dissuade the average American from indulging a taste for narrative fiction: novels like Richardson's *Clarissa Harlowe* and Fielding's *Tom Jones* helped feed the largely middle-class hunger for stories of manners, adventure, travel, and seduction (Hart 53–56).

Like fiction, the drama also benefitted from demographic and social changes. With the growth of cities and more widespread literacy came a rise in the number of theatres built, plays produced, and actors employed. By the late 1780s there were two permanent touring groups in America, as well as numerous travelling troupes from abroad. Owing again to suspicions about the degenerate influence of the stage, producers usually billed plays as delightful instruction. Shakespeare's *Othello*, for instance, was advertised in 1761 as "a series of MORAL DIALOGUES, in Five Parts, Depicting the evil effects of jealousy, and other bad passions, and proving that happiness can only spring from the pursuit of virtue" (Wood 281). But those proscriptions against drama began to fade after the Revolution, as a rising middle class of educated people came to recognize that entertainment was not necessarily a waste of time. When a touring company in Philadelphia petitioned the city council for a permanent theatre in 1788, a citizens' committee countered with the usual charges that the actors were purveyors of licentiousness and depravity, on a par with "jugglers, mountebanks, ropedancers, and other immoral and irreligious entertainments" (Wood 286). Over those objections, and despite some high ticket prices and the tendency of some audiences to pelt players with garbage, Philadelphia got its stage in 1794 (Nye 264). Apparently the ropedancers never caught on.

American writers were cheered by all of this interest in literature, and well they should have been, for in a country known for its practicality, widening appreciation of the fine arts was no small revelation. Still, a quick look back at the lists of popular books of the era indicates a problem much on the mind of literary artists in the new United States. With the exception of the *Federalist Papers* in 1787, Paine's tract *Common Sense*, and the poem *M'Fingal* by John Trumbull—more about that poem in a minute—citizens of the new nation were stocking their libraries with books by British and continental authors. The irony was inescapable. The nation that had just won its political independence had yet to establish its independence in the literary arts. Ralph Waldo Emerson would write in his essay "The Poet" some fifty years later, "America is a poem in our eyes; its ample geography dazzles the imagination, and it will not wait long for metres." But America was still waiting in the 1780s, and the need for a national literature commensurate with our political greatness had never seemed more acute.

Please do not misunderstand me on this point. As any of my students will attest, I will argue long and hard that a vibrant literary life existed well before the American Revolution. Since the 1630s the colonists in the New World, especially those in New England, had read and written journals, sermons, treatises, autobiographies, histories, and a remarkable body of poetry in celebration of the American landscape and the possibilities of life in the wilderness. Much of this seemed dated, though, by the revolutionary era, and much more of it—particularly the poetry—lay unpublished in commonplace books and family Bibles until modern scholars recovered and printed it in this century. In any event, I would argue, patriotic and political considerations, not aesthetic ones, made colonial American literature decidedly unsuited to national needs. Just as the constitution helped to define the character of the new nation, so poetry, prose, and drama were enlisted into the service of national self-definition. That most tireless of American promoters, Noah Webster, gave voice to the national aim in the preface to his American speller, published in 1783:

> This country must in some future time, be as distinguished by the superiority of her literary improvements, as she is already by the liberality of her civil and ecclesiastical constitutions. Europe is grown old in folly, corruption and tyranny—in that country laws are perverted, manners are licentious, literature is declining and human nature debased. For America in her infancy to adopt the present maxims of the old world, would be to stamp the wrinkles of decrepit age upon the bloom of youth. . . . It is the business of *Americans* to select the wisdom of all nations, as the basis of her constitution . . . [and] to add superior dignity to this infant Empire and to human nature. (Webster 14–15)

Webster's sentiments were echoed up and down the thirteen colonies, in one form or another, after the Revolution. The *Columbian Magazine* of Philadelphia, one of the most popular of its day, bore this inscription: "America! with Peace and Freedom blest, / Pant for true Fame, and scorn inglorious rest; / Science invites, urged by the Voice divine, / Exert thy self, 'till every Art be thine" (Mott, *American Magazines* 95). A new age called for a new literature, and called loudly.

19

As we might expect, the literature produced in response to that call was patriotic, hortatory, and overwhelmingly defensive. At its worst it was versified warfare, a refighting of the Revolution. The most popular American poem of the day was *M'Fingal*, a mock-epic in four parts by John Trumbull, first published in 1776. The title character, a Tory buffoon named Squire M'Fingal, is one of the great windbags of American literature. In the poem he argues for the divine right of kings, the sanctity of British rule, and the necessary failure of the American cause. His opposite number, an American patriot named Honorius, compares the British empire to a senile old woman and calls the Tories cowards:

> Hie homeward from the glorious field;
> There turn the wheel, the distaff wield;
> Act what ye are, nor dare to stain
> The warrior's arms with touch profane:
> There beg your more heroic wives
> To guard your children and your lives;
> Beneath their aprons find a screen,
> Nor dare to mingle more with men. (Trumbull 150)

Revolutionary poetry, you see, was not marred by an excess of sophisticated thought. In cantos three and four of *M'Fingal*, patriots and loyalists do battle around a liberty-pole on which has been raised an American flag. M'Fingal gets brained by a shovel-wielding colonial, is tarred and feathered by a frenzied mob of patriots, and has a vision of the American victory that dovetails almost exactly with the actual military history of the war. That Trumbull waited until the end of the Revolution to publish this final part of the poem may tell us something about his own confidence in the American cause. But there is no doubt in the poem about who is the villain, who the hero. Appealing as it does to a flag-waving sense of national belligerence, *M'Fingal* was a runaway best-seller during the War of Independence and well into the 1780s.

After the war, however, British-bashing in literature took a new turn. Its political independence won, the new United States still suffered from a kind of intellectual inferiority complex. And this, I believe, was the impetus for much of the literature produced in the post-revolutionary period. Embedded in our national psyche, then and now, is the idea that we are a "city upon a hill": the eyes of the world are upon us. And in the world's eyes in the 1780s the new nation had yet to prove itself, in science, philosophy, or literature. Particularly galling were the charges of a French naturalist, Georges Louis Leclerc de Buffon. In his forty-four-volume *Natural History*, completed in 1788, Buffon advanced the theory of the degeneration of species in the New World. America's animals, he argued, were smaller, less powerful, and not as smart as their European counterparts—

and, said Buffon, "man is here no exception to the general rule" (Buffon 18:146). An angry Thomas Jefferson, no mean scientist himself, answered Buffon by sending him the skeleton of an enormous North American moose. But the charges of American lack of literary genius were much harder to refute. And so our writers took it upon themselves to create a literature with American themes built from American materials in an American language, an original literature uncorrupted by the legacy of Europe.

But these were Englishmen, after all, born under the Union Jack and steeped in the literature of the Commonwealth. Severing artistic ties with the Old World was easier said than done. Complicating the task were the prevailing standards of neoclassical criticism, the rules of order, propriety, balance, and respect for literary tradition. Breaking with the king was one thing; breaking with Shakespeare, Milton, Pope, and Swift was quite another. To slavishly imitate European literature would prove that Americans had no talent; but to cut the ties completely would show that we had no taste.

The road to a national literature, in short, was a rough one to travel, for our writers in the 1780s labored under a set of contradictory demands: assert our independence from European standards of art, prove our superiority by those same standards, and everywhere define in literature the new national character—a real dilemma.

I would like to take a look now at three important American works of 1787, the year that the Constitution was approved, to assess how well those demands were met.

Letters from an American Farmer was published, oddly enough, by a Frenchman, not a native-born American, who was only nominally a farmer. Hector St. Jean de Crèvecoeur was an interesting character, uniquely suited to observe American life and to report on it to the world. Born in Normandy, France, he spent his youth in England and Canada, enlisting there in the French militia during the French and Indian War in the late 1750s. He was badly wounded during the Battle of Quebec in 1759 and left Canada for New York later the same year. Throughout much of the 1760s he led the adventurer's life, working as a surveyor and an Indian trader, travelling up and down the Atlantic Coast and west into the Ohio Valley, becoming a naturalized citizen of New York along the way. In 1769 he settled down, married, and bought a 120-acre "gentleman's farm" in rural Orange County, north of New York, where he began to write essays and sketches about the American colonies, his adopted home. During the American Revolution he gathered these essays for publication abroad, but as he tried to sail from New York he was captured as a suspected spy and jailed by the British. Nearly a year later he made it to London, where a shorter version of his book appeared in 1782. While he was overseas Indians raided Orange Country, burning his home and murdering his wife. What was left of the family was reunited in France in 1783; Crèvecoeur had by this time secured the American consulship from the French government. He continued to write about America, publishing a final, expanded version of the *Letters from an American Farmer* in Paris in 1787. Reduced to poverty during the French Revolution, Crèvecoeur never returned to the United States. He died in Germany in 1813.

My purpose in spending so much time on Crèvecoeur's life is to contrast him with the "American farmer" who supposedly wrote the letters. In fact, these were no letters at all, but carefully wrought essays on life and manners in the United States. And the observations are made not, strictly speaking, by Crèvecoeur—adventurer, cosmopolitan, political appointee—but by a narrator Crèvecoeur created specially for his purposes: an honest, peace-loving tiller of the soil named James. James is what literary critics call a persona—a mask or identity an author uses to tell a story or represent a point of view. This humble narrator, so the fiction goes, undertakes to educate an English friend with "local and unadorned information" about the New World (Crèvecoeur 3). Through James, Crèvecoeur paints a picture of eighteenth-century American life from the slave-stalls of Charleston, South Carolina, to the whaling villages of Massachusetts, and especially the agrarian life of the middle Atlantic states. Crèvecoeur's book is a charming, detailed, imaginative ode to rural America, a land threatened by corruption yet the best world of all possible ones. As James admits in letter 2, entitled "The Situation, Feelings, and Pleasures of an American Farmer," there is evil everywhere, but less of it here. "I therefore rest satisfied," he says, "and thank God that my lot is to be an American farmer, instead of a Russian boor, or an Hungarian peasant" (Crèvecoeur 17).

What gives coherence to the book, besides its consistent point of view and narration, is the third chapter, entitled "What Is an American?" In this, the most famous section of the *Letters*, James presents a sales pitch for the nation, aimed at prospective European immigrants:

> No sooner does an European arrive, no matter of what condition, than his eyes are opened upon the fair prospect; he hears his language spoken, he retraces many of his own country manners, he perpetually hears the names of families and towns with which he is acquainted; he sees happiness and prosperity in all places disseminated; he meets with hospitality, kindness, and plenty everywhere; he beholds hardly any poor, he seldom hears of punishments and executions; and he wonders at the elegance of our towns, those miracles of industry and freedom. He cannot admire enough our rural districts, our con-

venient roads, good taverns, and our many accommodations;
he involuntarily loves a country where everything is so lovely.
(Crèvecoeur 52)

More to the point, though, James tries to pin down the new American
character:

> What then is the American, this new man? He is either an
> European, or the descendant of an European, hence that strange
> mixture of blood, which you will find in no other country. I
> could point out to you a family whose grandfather was an
> Englishman, whose wife was Dutch, whose son married a French
> woman, and whose present four sons have now four wives of
> different nations. He is an American, who, leaving behind him
> all his ancient prejudices and manners, receives new ones from
> the new mode of life he has embraced, the new government
> he obeys, and the new rank he holds. He becomes an American
> by being received in the broad lap of our great Alma Mater.
> Here individuals of all nations are *melted* into a new race of
> men, whose labours and posterity will one day cause great
> changes in the world. Americans are the western pilgrims,
> who are carrying along with them that great mass of arts,
> sciences, vigour, and industry which began long since in the
> east; they will finish the great circle. (Crèvecoeur 39)

The *Letters of an American Farmer* pinpoints perhaps the two most
powerful myths of American self-concept—the melting pot and a sort
of cultural manifest destiny. But as a definition, James's answer is
slippery stuff; the new American is identified more by what he is
not than by what he is. This approach is understandable since the
new nation was still unsure of what exactly it had become, but nevertheless it is a picture of America more imaginary than real. George
Washington, who recommended the *Letters* to European readers, admitted that Crèvecoeur's portrait was "embellished with rather too
flattering circumstances" (Washington 29:522); a British critic sniffed
that the *Letters* "exceedingly exaggerated the excellencies of the United
States" (Philbrick 162); a twentieth-century editor of Crèvecoeur has
called it "delightful literature, but fanciful sociology" (Lewisohn vii).

Fanciful sociology—precisely the point, I think, for Crèvecoeur's
aim in the *Letters* was not to reflect but to *create* a version of America and its people. Ironically, the book was never a best-seller in
this country; after its first American edition in 1793, it was not
reprinted here for more than a century. But Europeans loved it: it
was reprinted or translated in Dublin (1782), Belfast (1783), Leipzig
(1784), and Leyden (1784), in addition to a second British edition in
1783 and four versions of Crèvecoeur's French text in 1784 and 1785
before the final version of 1787. Probably more than any other single
work, Crèvecoeur's shaped the European view of America in the 1780s.

Unlike Crèvecoeur, our second author, Joel Barlow, was a thorough-going Yankee born in Connecticut, educated at Yale, and for a brief time a soldier in the Revolutionary Army. After the war he married, founded a short-lived literary magazine, then studied law and was admitted to the bar. But like many educated men of his time, he had always been a dabbler in poetry. In the 1780s Barlow became part of a literary circle known today as the Connecticut Wits: urbane, largely conservative young writers whose ambition, frankly, outstripped their talents. Answering the call for a national literature, Barlow set out to create an American epic, an *Iliad* for the new United States. In 1787 he published his epic, an enormous historical poem in nine books called the *Vision of Columbus*.

The frame of the poem—that is, the situation that gives it shape—is that Columbus, languishing in prison at the end of his life, is visited by an angel who consoles him with a vision of the future greatness of the American continents. And what a sweeping vision it is! Books 2, 3, and 4 recount the history of the Incas in Peru; in books 5 and 6 Barlow turns to early settlement in North America and a poetic version of the American Revolution; in books 7 through 9 the visionary angel presents Columbus with an overview of America's destiny in commerce, the arts, science, and morality.

Barlow is at his best when he recreates historical scenes. For instance, consider his version of a night ambush during the American Revolution:

> So rush the raging files, and sightless close,
> In plunging strife, with fierce conflicting foes;
> They reach, they strike, they struggle o'er the slain,
> Deal heavier blows, and strow with death the plain;
> Ranks crush on ranks, with equal slaughter gored,
> While dripping streams, from every lifted sword,
> Stain the thin carnaged hosts; who still maintain,
> With mutual shocks, the vengeance of the plain. (Barlow 2:289)

Like Crèvecoeur, he prophesies that America shall fulfill the promise of civilization:

> Each orient realm, with former pride of earth,
> Where men and science drew their ancient birth,
> Shall soon behold, on this enlightened coast,
> Their fame transcended and their glory lost.
> That train of arts, that graced mankind before,
> Warm'd the glad sage or taught the Muse to soar,
> Here with superior sway their progress trace,
> And aid the triumphs of thy filial race. (Barlow 2:303)

You will forgive me if I quote no more of the *Vision of Columbus*; in fact, you might thank me. It really is awful stuff for the most part, contrived, learned in the worst ways, allusive, and windy. Barlow's biographer calls it "a dinosaur in the clay pits of literary history" (Ford 65). But Barlow does fulfill the demands of the new national literature in at least two ways: he creates a comprehensive sense of the American past, and he champions those distinctive elements of life on this shore—economic opportunity, lack of a political hierarchy, moderation in habits and beliefs—that would support America's rising glory in the future. In a manuscript draft of the poem completed as early as 1779, Barlow showed what he hoped to accomplish in the *Vision of Columbus:* "a Poem on the subject of America at large designed to exhibit the importance of this country in every point of view, as the noblest and most elevated part of the earth" (Ford 46). Barlow's American epic may not stir the imagination, but it was true to his plan and to the demands of his age for a poetry national in scope, patriotic in theme, and yet traditional in its literary form.

I need make no apologies for the third major American work of 1787, for unlike Barlow's *Vision* it remains readable—if rather quaint—two hundred years later. *The Contrast*, a comedy of manners written by the Boston-born Royall Tyler, was first performed at the John Street Theatre in New York City on April 16, 1787. It was not the first play written by an American (there had been perhaps forty before this, few of them actually performed), but it *was* the first native comedy produced professionally in this country. More important, it is really the first *good* drama written by a citizen of the United States, a witty spoof of morals and manners worthy to stand alongside the established British comedy of the day.

To summarize the story of *The Contrast* would be to ruin it; as with most domestic comedy, the wit, the double entendres, and the blunders count for more than the improbable thread of plot. In keeping with the comedic conventions of the eighteenth century, the characters are incompletely realized, merely types to be admired, jeered, or dismissed for their silliness. It is the contrasts between these stylized characters that give the play both its name and its appeal. At the heart of the play are three young ladies of upper-crust New York society, each being wooed—separately, of course—by a character named Billy Dimple. Dimple is a cad, clearly, and more: he is, to use the eighteenth-century term, a fop—a dandy, a phony, a womanizer, and an opportunist who models himself after the stylish characters he reads about in English novels. Billy Dimple's opposite is Colonel Manly, the brave, handsome brother of one of Billy's lady-friends. Billy has a servant who imitates his master's affectations: Jessamy. Manly, too, has a valet cast in his master's image: Jonathan, a homespun American rustic who entertains the love of his life by singing "Yankee Doodle." Dimple and Jessamy, the effeminate rogues, versus Manly and Jonathan, the sturdy men of honor—

the names say it all. True to the comedic genre, the schemers are found out in the end and the heroes get their ladies, amid a battle not of swords but of wits.

American audiences loved it. *The Contrast* was staged five times that first season in New York—not a bad run at all—and by the end of the century it had been put on in at least fifteen additional American cities; when Washington was inaugurated in 1789 it enjoyed another run in New York. The connection to Washington, in fact, was a natural one, for Colonel Manly of the play was in many ways a dramatic ringer for the first president. Part of the fun of the play is Manly's unrelenting Americanness. Billy Dimple appears on stage decked out in frills and lace; Manly wears a sword given him for bravery by Lafayette. But Manly conquers by force of his character: he has drawn this sword, he tells us, only "in the service of my country, and in private life, on the only occasion where a man is justified in drawing his sword, in defence of a lady's honour" (Act V, sc. 2). Manly worries for the fate of the country he has fought to create, worries that the creeping spread of British "luxury" will weaken its character; in Act III he even gives a timely plug for federal unity under the Constitution.

Dimple, on the other hand, is positively un-American in his attempt to imitate British fashion and morals. In Billy Dimple American literature found its first great exemplar of the corruption of the Old World, the sham and double-dealing and moral decay that Noah Webster had warned about in the preface to his speller. To be sure, Dimple is an unfair type, but to the audience that watched *The Contrast* in 1787 he was the personification of European values most suited to their needs. What better answer to the sneering charges about American degeneration than to show this Anglicized fop for what he was? Neither they nor we could have any doubt where the nobility lay. Have a character named Manly square off with one named Dimple, and you know who will win every time. As Manly says in the concluding scene, when he wins the hand of the fair lady Charlotte, "I have learned that probity, virtue, honour, though they should not have received the polish of Europe, will secure to an honest American the good graces of his fair countrywomen, and I hope, the applause of THE PUBLIC" (Act V, sc. 2). Manly's hope was not in vain; *The Contrast* remained the most famous American play for more than a century, almost timeless in its creation of national character. A literary declaration of independence, we might say, produced on the eve of the Constitution.

By examining these three works, I do not mean to suggest that they were the only important ones produced during the constitutional era. Indeed, this was a busy time in American literature. We could mention Jefferson's *Notes on the State of Virginia* (1785), a landmark study of American cultural geography; Phyllis Wheatley's *Poems on Various Subjects* (1773), the first poetry—in fact, the first book—published by a black American; or Philip Freneau's *Poems* (1786), which prefigured the age of Romantic literature in America. One of the first American novels, William Hill Brown's *Power of Sympathy*, would appear in 1789; the first novel by an American woman, *Charlotte Temple* by Susannah Rowson, in 1791. But the three works I have focused on here seem to me to represent American literary production firmly rooted in its time, a fair sampling of the best and the worst responses to the call for national literature.

Each of them sought to identify what was new in American subject matter; not surprisingly, the revolution and the native landscape were among the most popular themes. At the same time, each tried to conform to traditional genres: the occasional essay, the epic, the comedy of manners. And each presented a similar view of the American character as expansive, tolerant, courageous, even-handed, modest, and principled. The extent to which we as Americans have appropriated those characteristics, quite unfairly, as ours and ours alone, is perhaps evidenced by their persistence in popular literary heroes from that day forward: Cooper's Leatherstocking, Twain's Huck Finn, Wister's Virginian, Fitzgerald's Nick Carraway. American literature in the 1780s presented our face to the rest of the world—a world that doubted both the literary ability and the face it created. Like the framers of the Constitution, a document that mandated a kind of national unity out of diversity, American writers created in their work a composite set of values and assumptions that would come to be known as the American character—and we may well have spent the last two hundred years trying to measure up to the earliest models created for us. If most of us no longer read Crèvecoeur's *Letters*, Barlow's *Vision of Columbus*, or Tyler's *The Contrast*, it may have less to do with their literary merits than with the fact that the vision of us created there is today too internalized to need expression and too well accepted to need defense.

References

Barlow, Joel. *The Vision of Columbus: A Poem in Nine Books*. Hartford, 1787.

Buffon, Georges Louis Leclerc, comte de. *Histoire naturelle, générale et particulière*. 44 vols. Paris, 1749–1788.

Crèvecoeur, St. John de. *Letters from an American Farmer* (1783). New York: Dutton, 1957.

Ford, Arthur Lewis. *Joel Barlow*. New York: Twayne, 1971.

Lewisohn, Ludwig. Introduction to *Letters from an American Farmer* by St. John de Crèvecoeur. New York: Fox, Duffield, 1904.

Mott, Frank Luther. *Golden Multitudes: The Story of Best Sellers in the United States*. New York, Macmillan, 1947.

———. *A History of American Magazines, 1741–1850*. New York and London: D. Appleton, 1930.

Philbrick, Thomas. *St. John de Crèvecoeur*. New York: Twayne, 1970.

Trumbull, John. *Satiric Poems of John Trumbull*. Edited by Edwin T. Bowden. Austin: University of Texas Press, 1962.

Tyler, Royall. *The Contrast* (1790). Edited by James B. Wilbur. Boston: Houghton Mifflin, 1920.

Washington, George. *The Writings of George Washington*. Edited by John C. Fitzpatrick. Washington: United States Government Printing Office, 1931–44.

Webster, Noah. *A Grammatical Institute of the English Language*. Part I. Hartford, 1783.

Wood, Gordon S., ed. *The Rising Glory of America*. New York: George Braziller, 1971.

List of the Delegates Appointed by the States Represented in the Federal Convention

New Hampshire: *John Langdon, Nicholas Gilman*

Massachusetts: *Elbridge Gerry, Nathaniel Gorham, Rufus King, Caleb Strong*

Rhode Island: *No Appointment*

Connecticut: *William Samuel Johnson, Roger Sherman, Oliver Ellsworth*

New York: *Alexander Hamilton, John Lansing, Jr., Robert Yates*

New Jersey: *William Livingston, David Brearly, William Paterson, Jonathan Dayton, William Churchill Houston*

Pennsylvania: *Benjamin Franklin, Thomas Mifflin, Robert Morris, George Clymer, Thomas Fitzsimons, Jared Ingersoll, James Wilson, Gouverneur Morris*

Delaware: *George Read, Gunning Bedford, Jr., John Dickinson, Richard Basset, Jacob Broom*

Maryland: *James McHenry, Daniel of St. Thomas Jenifer, Daniel Carroll, John Francis Mercer, Luther Martin*

Virginia: *George Washington, Edmund Randolph, John Blair, James Madison, Jr., George Mason, George Wythe, James McClurg*

North Carolina: *Alexander Martin, William Richardson Davie, William Blount, Richard Dobbs Spaight, Hugh Williamson*

South Carolina: *John Rutledge, Charles Cotesworth Pinckney, Charles Pinckney, Pierce Butler*

Georgia: *William Few, Abraham Baldwin, William Pierce, William Houstoun*

"An Assembly of Demi-Gods": The Formation of the Constitution

Adapted for the Stage by Judy E. Yordon

Cast: Voice and Ben Franklin (Ed Strother), V.1 (Gary Simmers), V.2 (Marty Grubbs), V.3 (Tom Owen), V.4 (Tim Casto), V.5 (Steve Russell), Narrator (Jim Hardin)

Setting: Two lecterns, left and right of center; two platforms, one higher upstage and one in front of it; two square tables; six chairs. Curtain up. Lights up when Ed is down center. Leave house lights on.

Voice: On this occasion, both Washington's birthday and the bicentennial year of the founding of the Constitution, it seems only "necessary and proper" that we recreate that turbulent time when our system of government was being formulated. We offer for your edification and entertainment a docu-drama starring a present-day George Washington who, despite his rather minimal participation as president of the actual Convention, has agreed to be our narrator this evening. Although much of what follows consists of the exact words spoken or thought at the Convention, often history is adjusted to fit a dramatic structure. Now transport yourselves back two hundred years and observe at first hand how our government was shaped.

The Convention was the result of the following mandate from Congress:

"Resolved that in the opinion of Congress it is expedient that on the second Monday in May next, a Convention of delegates who shall have been appointed by the several states be held in Pennsylvania for the sole and express purpose of revising the Articles of Confederation and reporting to Congress and the several legislatures such alterations and provisions as shall when agreed to in Congress and confirmed by the states render the federal constitution adequate to the exigencies of Government and the preservation of the Union." (Slowly take out house lights)

30

Quiet please, Mr. George Washington now approaches the lectern.

Narr: When delegates from almost every state convened in Philadelphia in 1787, we were—in theory—setting out to "revise" the Articles of Confederation, but, in fact, we began to draw up a new framework for government, and after four hundred hours of debate what emerged was the Constitution. (Cast assembles, talking among themselves.) Let's meet the leading delegates responsible for the formation of this new centralized system of government.

V.2: Gunning Bedford. Attorney general of Delaware. Very fat and impetuous; a "bold and nervous Speaker" who defends the small states. Attended Princeton with James Madison.

V.3: John Dickinson. Pale, scholarly lawyer, educated at the Middle Temple, London. Famous for his defense of American rights in *Letters from a Farmer in Pennsylvania* (1767–68); now semi-retired in Delaware.

Voice: Benjamin Franklin. World-famous octogenarian of Philadelphia—printer, scientist, diplomat. "He snatched lightning from Heaven and the sceptre from tyrants." Supports a strong Union, envisions a continental republic.

V.3: Oliver Ellsworth. Tall, successful Connecticut lawyer and businessman, who has a habit of talking to himself. A moderate nationalist with a sure instinct for compromise.

V.4: Elbridge Gerry. Thin, dapper merchant from Marblehead, Massachusetts. Worried-looking, veering between republicanism and nationalism, yet sensitive to slights; stubborn in his views of the moment.

V.2: Nathaniel Gorham. Likable Boston merchant who leans toward nationalism. Son of a packet-boat operator, trained as a mechanic; engaged in privateering during the Revolution.

V.5: Alexander Hamilton. Brilliant nationalist from New York, eager for the establishment of a "high-toned" government but discouraged by presence of anti-nationalist colleagues. A short, slender man with mobile features; native of the British West Indies; very ambitious.

V.1: Rufus King. Good-looking young Massachusetts lawyer; converted to nationalism by his membership in Congress and the influence of Madison. Educated at Harvard; an effective speaker.

V.5: William Johnson. Modest, gracious Connecticut lawyer and scholar. Independently wealthy; shuns strife. Educated at Yale and Harvard; has just been named president of Columbia.

V.4: John Lansing. Wealthy New York landowner and lawyer. Speaker of the New York assembly and dependable lieutenant of antinationalist Governor Clinton. Handsome, hospitable.

V.1: Luther Martin. Carelessly dressed, broad-shouldered Marylander, with hair cropped short and florid complexion. Violently antinationalist; a long-winded orator known as the "reprobate genius" or wild man of the Convention.

V.4: James Madison. "A small man, quiet, somewhat precise in manner, pleasant, fond of conversation, with a . . . mixture of ease and dignity." A Virginian with a deep knowledge of ancient constitutions, also a sly sense of humor; leader of the nationalists.

V.2: George Mason. Independent, outspoken Virginia planter-aristocrat. A romantic republican, author of the Virginia Declaration of Rights; enemy of slavery and centralized government.

V.3: Gouverneur Morris. "The Tall Boy"—a large, genial, personable man with a peg leg, a strong nationalist from Pennsylvania. Gay, witty, a favorite with the ladies; steeped in French literature and an excellent writer.

V.2: Robert Morris. Hearty, thick-necked Philadelphia businessman known as the Financier of the Revolution. Hosts George Washington during the Convention; faces financial ruin and debtors' prison in the future.

V.5: William Paterson. A short, stubborn Irishman; attorney general of New Jersey, revolutionary veteran. Determined to protect states' rights, though willing to accept a moderate nationalism that does not infringe upon those rights.

V.4: Charles Cotesworth Pinckney. South Carolina lawyer-planter; distinguished general during the Revolution, an aide to Washington. Educated at Oxford and the Middle Temple, London. Genial, imposing; highly regarded in South Carolina.

V.1: Charles Pinckney. Second cousin to General Pinckney. A dedicated nationalist, lawyer, prominent member of Congress. Youthful, but wishes to be thought still younger than his twenty-nine years; handsome, somewhat vain.

V.3: Edmund Randolph. Handsome, dark-haired governor of Virginia. A moderate nationalist, but concerned about his popularity and political standing at home. Educated at William and Mary.

V.5: John Rutledge. Proud, imperious South Carolina planter-aristocrat. Activist-leader in his state during the Revolution. Educated at the Middle Temple, London.

V.1: Roger Sherman. Lean, sharp-nosed, canny New Englander; jack-of-all-trades who has risen from a shoemaker's to a judge's bench in Connecticut. Inclines slightly toward antinationalism, but is pragmatic. Called "cunning as the Devil" by an opponent.

V.4: Hugh Williamson. Scientist, physician (M.D. from Utrecht), surgeon-general of the North Carolina forces during the Revolution. A very versatile, genial man of the world; a strong nationalist.

V.1: James Wilson. "The Caledonian" [Scotsman]—stout, ruddy, precise. Educated at St. Andrews University, Scotland, before coming to Pennsylvania as a country lawyer. Powerful champion of the nationalists; noted for his reasoning ability.

Narr: And I, of course, am George Washington. The man who controls his strong feelings, lives by maxims of truth and honor, and hates to be the object of criticism. The story of the making of the Constitution—which is what we are about to tell, is one of the most dramatic in American history. On that gray May 25 (it turned out not to be the second Monday in May), 1787, the delegates began arriving with various agendas and points of view. I even hesitated to attend, feeling that the confederation would fail, would be "shadow without substance," but I am glad I was wrong. Fifty-five men were sent from all but one of the thirteen states, although New Hampshire's delegation arrived late. Rhode Island . . .

V.5 (as A. Hamilton): Rogue Island, you mean.

Narr: . . . stayed aloof. Only thirty of the fifty-five men were constant in their attendance through that long, hot, humid summer in Philadelphia.

V.1 (as L. Martin): Hot? Humid? While liberty was at stake in that east room, we sweated physically as well as mentally. We couldn't even open a window to relieve the desperate heat because that would let in the flies buzzing angrily outside. At the most critical stage of the Convention, the crashing thunderstorms that briefly cooled the afternoon did not break.

Narr: Thirty-nine signed the final document. It seemed to me at the time to be a "miracle" that the delegates from so many different states in their manners, circumstances, and prejudices should unite in forming a system of national government so little liable to well-founded objections. Thomas Jefferson, minister to France, who was unable to attend the Convention because he was kept overseas by assignment, called the delegates, and with some justice, "an assembly of demi-gods." Let's listen to some of the proceedings. (The men vie for recognition.) The chair recognizes James Madison of Virginia.

V.4 (as James Madison): Our object, as I see it, is to secure the public good and private rights against the danger of such a faction and at the same time to preserve the spirit and form of popular government. I propose that there be a legislature of two houses. The lower would be elected by the people and the upper elected by the lower. Both houses—one directly, the other indirectly—would thus reflect population rather than statehood. (The men vie for recognition again).

V.2 (not waiting to be recognized as G. Bedford): If the large states dissolve the Confederation, the small ones will find some foreign ally who will take them by the hand and do them justice.

Narr (with renewed authority): The chair recognizes John Dickinson of Delaware.

V.3 (as J. Dickinson): I am not surprised that Mr. Madison would devise a "Virginia Plan" that would favor the larger states. His state of Virginia excluding Kentucky has 750,000 people, while my constituents number 60,000. The small states would sooner submit to a foreign power than be deprived of an equality of suffrage in both branches of the legislature, and thereby be thrown under the domination of the large states. Is this what Mr. Madison means by "the spirit and form of popular government"? (Vie for attention.)

Narr: The chair recognizes William Paterson of New Jersey.

V.5 (as W. Paterson): I propose an alternative plan because I believe that the Virginia Plan will throw the states into hotchpot! Let us have a legislature of one house, elected by the states regardless of population, and with a plural executive elected by the Congress. (Vie for attention.)

Narr: As the debate continued, I realized that the Convention would last some time. I thus wrote home requesting that my new umbrella be sent and inquiring about the thinning of the carrots, which were too thick. The chair now recognizes Benjamin Franklin.

Voice as B. Franklin: The small progress we have made after four or five weeks close attendance and continual reasonings with each other . . . is methinks a melancholy proof of the imperfection of the human understanding. We indeed seem to feel our own want of political wisdom, since we have been running about in search of it. We have gone back to ancient history for models of government. And we have viewed modern states all 'round Europe, but find none of their constitutions suitable to our circumstances. In this situation how has it happened, sir, that we have not hitherto once thought of humbly applying to the Father of lights to illuminate our understandings? I have lived, sir, a long time, and the longer I live, the more convincing proofs I see of this truth—*that God governs in the affairs of men*. I therefore beg leave to move—that henceforth prayers imploring the assistance of heaven, and its blessings on our deliberations, be held in this assembly every morning before we proceed to business, and that one or more of the clergy of this city be requested to officiate in that service.

V.1 (as R. Sherman): I second the motion.

V.5 (as A. Hamilton): I think we should give this proposal serious consideration. I worry that the public will view this action as a sign of embarrassments and dissensions within the Convention.

V. 4 (as H. Williamson): I do not think that we have money with which to pay a minister.

V. 3 (as R. Morris): Move adjournment.

Voice as B. Franklin (as though writing in his journal): Thought prayers unnecessary!

Narr: The next day, the crisis continued. The delegates were now in the eye of the storm. On July 2, a motion that each state have one vote in the Senate received a tie vote, 5–5. Thus the motion failed, but the large and small states remained deadlocked. Within eight days the disaffected states' rights delegates from New York would walk out, leaving only eleven states represented. Within two weeks William Paterson of New Jersey would propose that the whole Convention go home—without having written a constitution. Roger Sherman of Connecticut relieved the tension.

V.1 (as R. Sherman): We are now at a full stop, so I propose a compromise. Let us give the states equal representation in the Senate while maintaining the national principle—representation by population in the House. (The men talk among themselves, most pleased with this solution.)

Narr: This important compromise became known as The Great, the Connecticut, or the Sherman Compromise. It came after approximately one month of debate. It ultimately became the basis of the American government. It also saved the convention from dissolution. Important though it was, it was designed to meet a dilemma—the rivalry of great and small states—that was largely illusory. Maryland, a small state, and Virginia, a large one, shared on the Chesapeake a common economy of tobacco plantations and slave labor. (To delegates as well as to audience) What should be done about slavery in the constitution of a republic? (To audience) The issue was raised in July, uneasily compromised, then raised again in August. Another crisis threatened. But perhaps because the delegates were tiring, a compromise was accepted. The chair recognizes Edmund Randolph of Virginia.

V.3 (as E. Randolph): I propose that in the census a slave will count as three-fifths of a freeman. (V.4 as Madison violently objects. Narrator tries to maintain order.) Slaves imported from abroad can be taxed like other "goods"—but after 1800 . . .

Narr: —changed to 1808—

V.3 (cont. as E. Randolph): . . . the slave trade could be . . .

Narr: —and was—

V.3 (cont. as E. Randolph): . . . prohibited.

Narr: Could the delegates have done more? It is a moot question. Like Lincoln three-quarters of a century later, they placed the Union ahead of social reforms. To hold the southern states, the North had to give some ground. (But James Madison and George Mason of Virginia violently denounced slavery.) Also, even the strongest antislavery men, although they despised the institution, seem scarcely to have thought of the slaves themselves as persons and possible equals. However, they were so disturbed by the situation that they avoided using the words "slave" and "slavery" in the Constitution. Slaves were "Person[s] held to Service or Labour" or "all other Persons" (in addition to freemen). The fiery debates on slavery continued. The chair recognizes General Pinckney.

V.1 (as Pinckney): Blacks must be included in the rule of representation *equally* with the whites: and for that purpose I move that the words "three-fifths" be struck out.

Narr: Mr. Gerry.

V.2 (as E. Gerry): It seems to me that three-fifths of them was to say the least the full proportion that could be admitted.

Narr: The chair recognizes Nathaniel Gorham.

V.2 (as N. Gorham): This ratio was fixed by Congress as a rule of taxation. Then it was urged by the delegates representing the states having slaves that the blacks were still more inferior to freemen. At present when the ratio of representation is to be established, we are assured that they are equal to freemen. The arguments on the former occasion had convinced me that three-fifths was pretty near the just proportion and we should vote according to the same opinion now.

Narr: James Wilson.

V.1 (as J. Wilson): I do not understand on what principle the admission of blacks in the proportion of three-fifths could be explained. Are they admitted as citizens? Then why are they not admitted on an equality with white citizens? Are they admitted as property? Then why is not other property admitted into the computation? These are the difficulties, however, which I think must be overruled by the necessity of compromise.

Narr: The chair recognizes Gouverneur Morris from Pennsylvania.

V.3 (as G. Morris): I am compelled to declare myself reduced to the dilemma of doing injustice to the southern states or to human nature, and I must therefore do it to the former. For I could never agree to give such encouragement to the slave trade as would be given by allowing them a representation for their Negroes.

Narr: Mr. Pinckney.

V.1 (as C. Pinckney): I move to amend Mr. Randolph's motion so as to make "blacks equal to the whites in the ratio of representation." This, my friends, is nothing more than justice. The blacks are the laborers, the peasants of the southern states: they are as productive of pecuniary resources as those of the northern states.

Narr: The speeches above were given in July, when the preliminary decision about how slaves were to be counted was made. In August the subject came up again in the Committee of Detail's rough draft of the complete Constitution. The delegates went through the rough draft article by article. A bit later, the question of allowing or prohibiting the importation of more slaves was discussed. The chair recognizes John Rutledge from South Carolina.

V.5 (as J. Rutledge): Religion and humanity have nothing to do with the question of the slave trade. Interest alone is the governing principle with nations. The true question at present is whether the southern states shall or shall not be parties to the Union. If the northern states consult their interest, they will not oppose the increase of slaves, which will increase the commodities of which they will become the carrier.

Narr: Mr. Pinckney.

V.1 (as C. Pinckney): South Carolina can never receive the plan if it prohibits the slave trade. In every proposed extension of the powers of the Congress, that state has expressly and watchfully excepted that of meddling with the importation of Negroes. If the states be all left at liberty on this subject, South Carolina may perhaps by degrees do of herself what is wished.

Narr: Yes, Colonel Mason.

V.2 (as G. Mason): This infernal traffic originated in the avarice of British merchants. The British government constantly checked the attempts of Virginia to put a stop to it. The present question concerns not the importing states alone but the whole Union. Maryland and Virginia have already prohibited the importation of slaves expressly. North Carolina has done the same in substance. All this would be in vain if South Carolina and Georgia are at liberty to import. The western people are already calling out for slaves for their new lands, and will fill that country with slaves if they can be got through South Carolina and Georgia. Slavery discourages arts and manufacturers. The poor despise labor when performed by slaves. They prevent the immigration of whites, who really enrich and strengthen a country. They produce the most pernicious effect on manners. Every master of slaves is born a petty tyrant. They bring the judgment of heaven on a country. I hold it essential in every point of view that the general government have power to prevent the increase of slavery.

Narr: George Mason's denunciation of slavery was made a week before the final compromise on August 29, which allowed importation of slaves to continue until 1808. Mason's speech had little or no effect. In addition to slavery, another problem the delegates wrestled with early was that of the chief executive. They couldn't agree on how long he should be in office, whether he could be reelected, and especially how he should be chosen in the first place. But they quickly decided that he should be an independent and powerful figure. The enterprising classes represented in the Convention were tired of the muddling-through ways of the weak Confederation. It was assumed that the first president would be myself, whom I hoped all trusted.

V.2: But should the president oversee the laws,

V.4: make high appointments (to be confirmed by the Senate),

V.5: and be commander-in-chief of the armed forces?

V.1: Should he veto bills passed by Congress if he considered them bad,

V.3: and should he make his opponents muster a two-thirds majority to override his veto?

Narr: At least one delegate thought the president might order the armed forces into action in an emergency without consulting Congress. Not all the powers and limitations of the presidency were spelled out; an energetic president would have more influence than an inactive one. In general, the balance between an independent executive and Congress resembled that between an eighteenth-century English king and Parliament. Gouverneur Morris developed the idea of a strong executive:

V.3 (as G. Morris): It is necessary to take into one view all that relates to the establishment of the executive; on the due formation of which must depend the efficacy and utility of the Union among the present and future states. It has been a maxim in political science that republican government is not adapted to a large extent of country, because the energy of the executive magistracy cannot reach the extreme parts of it. Our country is an extensive one. We must either then renounce the blessings of the Union, or provide an executive with sufficient vigor to pervade every part of it. One great object of the executive is to control the legislature. The legislature will continually seek to aggrandize and perpetuate themselves and will seize those critical moments produced by war, invasion, or convulsion for that purpose. It is necessary then that the executive magistrate should be the guardian of the people, even of the lower classes, against legislative tyranny, against the great and the wealthy who in the course of things will necessarily compose the legislative body. Wealth tends to corrupt the mind and to nourish its love of power, and to stimulate it to oppression. History proves this to be the spirit of the opulent. The executive therefore ought to be so constituted as to be the great protector of the mass of the people.

Narr: Later the Convention rejected a requirement that candidates for president be rich men worth at least $100,000. The young South Carolina aristocrat Charles Pinckney made this proposal; Benjamin Franklin rebutted it—expressing the democratic sentiments of the majority.

Voice as Franklin: I dislike everything that tends to debase the spirit of the common people. If honesty is often the companion of wealth, and if poverty is exposed to peculiar temptation, it is not less true that the possession of property increases the desire of more property. Some of the greatest rogues I was ever acquainted with, were the richest rogues. We should remember the character which the Scripture requires in rulers, that they should be men hating covetousness. This Constitution will be much read and attended to in Europe, and if it should betray a great partiality to the rich, will not only hurt us in the esteem of the most liberal and enlightened men there, but discourage the common people from removing to this country.

Narr: The rough draft of the Constitution gave Congress the power to declare war. There was a brief discussion of this clause, and the question of whether the president by himself could declare war was brought up. This issue foreshadowed a twentieth-century conflict between the president and the Congress. The chair recognizes Mr. Pinckney.

V.1 (as C. Pinckney): I oppose vesting this power in the legislature. Its proceedings would be too slow. It would meet but once a year. The House of Representatives would be too numerous for such deliberations. The Senate would be the best depository, being more acquainted with foreign affairs.

Narr: The chair recognizes John Rutledge of South Carolina.

V.5 (as J. Rutledge): The objections against the legislature lie in great degree against the Senate. I am for vesting the power in the president, who will have all the requisite qualities, and will not make war but when the nation will support it.

Narr: Mr. Sherman.

V.1 (as Sherman): The executive should be able to repel and not to commence war.

Narr: Mr. Gerry.

V.4 (as Gerry): I never expected to hear in a republic a motion to empower the executive alone to declare war!

V.2 (as Mason): I am for clogging rather than facilitating war. I am for facilitating peace.

Narr: The Convention created a strong president, but its members were as baffled as Congressmen and commentators today over how to elect him.

V.1: By popular vote?

V.2: By a complicated electoral college?

V.5: By Congress itself?

Narr: At first the delegates were in favor of having Congress do the job.

V.3: But might that not lead to deals between candidates and the legislators?

V.4: Wouldn't it violate the principle of the separation of powers and make the executive dependent on the legislature?

Narr: One aristocrat—

V.3: Gouverneur Morris.

Narr: and one democrat—

V.1: James Wilson.

Narr: —put their heads together and astounded everyone by suggesting that—

V.1 and V.3: —the people choose the president.

V.1 (as Wilson): Then he would represent the people against special interests of the wealthy class, which might be influential in Congress.

Narr: But the delegates would not go that far toward democracy. The American Revolution had opened the doors of government to the people, but their full participation still lay in the future.

V.3 (as Dickinson): Then what about a kind of Mr. America contest? Let each state nominate its "best citizen," and then Congress could select one of the thirteen as president.

Narr: As you might expect, this proposal aroused little enthusiasm. Then in despair or in a moment of cynicism, James Wilson suggested:

V.1 (as Wilson): What if a handful of members of Congress be chosen— "by lot"! These electors could then choose a president.

Narr: At last, after casting sixty ballots on the subject without reaching an agreement, the Convention threw up its hands and called on a Committee of Eleven to settle "postponed matters." This committee recommended that each state legislature provide a certain number of electors—the same number as the state's Representatives and Senators combined. These electors would meet and choose a president, but if no candidate received a majority of votes, the Senate would choose from among the five highest. A weary Convention accepted this solution—except that it gave the House instead of the Senate the right to decide an inconclusive election, with each state delegation there having just one vote. This is the basis of our system today. Other issues discussed were

V.1: "Is the Vice President necessary,"

V.2: "Religion,"

V.3: and "Power to the People."

Narr: After the delegates had revised the rough draft of the Constitution, they handed it over to a Committee of Style. (V. 3 works with everyone's scripts.) Gouverneur Morris did most of the polishing of the Constitution for this committee. He used—

V.3: —the plain, common language of mankind.

Narr: One of his happiest changes was in the preamble. The rough draft read:

V.5: We the People of the States of New Hampshire, Massachusetts (keep reading the other names under Narrator's following line: Virginia, Georgia)

Narr: naming them all,

V.5: do ordain, declare, and establish the following Constitution:

Narr: Morris changed this to

V.3: We the People of the United States—

Narr: —and added—

V.3: in order to form a more perfect Union, to establish Justice, insure domestic Tranquillity, provide for the common defense, promote the general Welfare, and secure the Blessings of Liberty to ourselves and our Posterity, do ordain and establish this Constitution—

Narr: So the Convention neared its goal. But as it did so, a few extreme republicans became more and more distressed.

V.2: Why was there no discussion of a bill of rights to protect the people? Why all the emphasis on the powers of the Senate, of the president, of the Supreme Court?

Narr: Everything was being done—as the fiery Patrick Henry was soon to cry out—*against* the "spirit of republicanism," *against* the "genius of democracy"! The complaints of the three dissenters—

V.3: Mr. Randolph.

V.4: Mr. Gerry.

V.2: Mr. Mason.

Narr: —reached a crescendo during the final days of the Convention. They rose to explain why they could not sign the document.

V.4: We foresee a dangerous drift of the American Republic toward either monarchy or aristocracy.

V.2: An all-powerful president or an arrogant Senate would crush the liberties of the people.

Voice of Franklin (rises, the three dissenters sit, Franklin is aided by V.1 as Wilson): I confess that there are several parts of this constitution which I do not at present approve, but I am not sure I shall never approve them, for having lived long, I have experienced many instances of being obliged by better information, or fuller consideration, to change opinions even on important subjects. The older I grow, the more apt I am to doubt my own judgment and to pay more respect to the judgment of others. So, I agree to this Constitution with all its faults because I think a general government necessary for us, and there is no form of government but what may be a blessing to the people if well administered. I consent to this Constitution because I expect no better, and because I am not sure that it is not the best. On the whole, I cannot help expressing a wish that every member of the Convention who may still have objections to it would with me on this occasion doubt a little of his own infallibility, and put his name to this instrument. (V1 and V5 and Voice slowly approach Narrator and mime signing the document. V2, 3, 4, remain at tables.)

Narr: The Constitution was signed on the seventeenth day of September, 1787, by all the members except Mr. Randolph, Mr. Mason, and Mr. Gerry, and the Convention dissolved by an adjournment *sine die.*

Then the battle began with the formation of political parties. On one side were those who wanted a strong central or national government, and on the other side those who preferred the retention of power by the state governments. The ratification of the Constitution divided the country into Federalists (led by James Madison, Alexander Hamilton, and John Jay), who supported the new form of government, and the Antifederalists (led by George Mason and Elbridge Gerry), who opposed it.

Although there were differences among members of both parties, there were some points upon which most agreed. Some Federalists who approved of the Constitution—

V.5: felt that the new government was too strong and needed amending once ratification took place;

V.4: others believed that the new government was too weak.

V.5: Some thought that the president should be replaced by a king,

V.4: others that he should serve for life,

V.5: still others that he was already too strong;

V.4: many wanted the states to retain varying degrees of power;

V.5: a few wanted to abolish the states.

Narr: Like the opponents, the Antifederalists differed in opinion, but they too concurred in a few primary ideas.

V.2 (as G. Mason): All of them, for example, believed that the Constitution created too strong a government. A fundamental conviction of nearly all Antifederalists was that the Constitution established a national, not a federal, government, a consolidation of previously independent states into one, a transfer of sovereignty in which the states, once sovereign, would retain but a shadow of their former power.

Narr: The strategy of the opponents of the Constitution, the Antifederalists, was to delay the drive for quick ratification by the states.

V.2 (as G. Mason): They appealed to the fear of change, to state pride, to the suspicions of backwoods debtors that the wealthy classes of the seaboard would cheat them.

Narr: When Delaware ratified the Constitution on December 7, 1787, after only five days of debate in its convention, the Antifederalists cried that—

V.2 (as G. Mason): Delaware had "reaped the honor of having first surrendered the liberties of the people!"

V.2: George Mason left Philadelphia in an exceeding ill humor because none of his protests had been heeded.

V.4: Elbridge Gerry declared that he could never accept the Constitution unless a second convention were summoned to improve it.

Narr: On October 7, 1787, George Mason sent me a short paper containing his objections to the Constitution.

V.2 (as G. Mason): There is no declaration of rights; and, the laws of the general government being superior to the laws and constitutions of the several states, the declaration of rights in the separate states are no security. In the House there is not the substance, but the shadow only, of representation. The Senate have the power of altering all money bills, and the salaries of the officers of their own appointment. These, with their other great powers; their influence upon, and connection with, the supreme executive; their duration of office will enable them to accomplish what usurpations they please upon the rights and liberties of the people. The judiciary of the United States will absorb and destroy the judiciaries of the several states. There is no declaration of any kind for preserving the liberty of the press, the trial by jury in civil cases, nor against the danger of standing armies in time of peace.

Narr: The omission of a "declaration of rights" was nearly to prove the Achilles' heel of the Federalist cause. It was in vain that the Federalists replied that—

V.5 (as Hamilton): These rights could be taken for granted, they were guaranteed in the state constitutions, the Constitution left all powers it did not name in the hands of the people.

Narr: This would not satisfy the age of republicanism and the rights of man. Early in 1788 Elbridge Gerry jotted down the arguments against the Constitution that he had been voicing in Massachusetts. This numbered list was published as a pamphlet "by a Columbian Patriot." It was one of the most complete, yet concise summaries of the Antifederalist case. Some of his main points follow:

V.4: (1) The most sagacious advocates have not evinced the necessity of adopting this many headed monster [the Constitution]; of such motley mixture that its enemies cannot trace a feature of Democratic or Republican extract; nor have its friends the courage to denominate a monarchy, an aristocracy, or an oligarchy. (2) There is no security in the proffered system, either for the rights of conscience or the liberty of the press. (3) There are no well-defined limits of the judiciary powers. (4) The executive and the legislative are so dangerously blended as to give just cause of alarm.

Narr: The most philosophical *defense* of the Constitution was the work of Alexander Hamilton, James Madison, and John Jay. From October 1787 through 1788 their *Federalist* essays appeared in various New York newspapers. The *Federalist* became a classic; it is considered the most important single interpretation of the Constitution and has often been cited by the Supreme Court in its decisions.

Because they had something positive to offer, the Federalists gained early momentum. They needed ratification by nine states out of thirteen. By mid-January 1788 they had won in Delaware, New Jersey, Georgia, Connecticut, and Pennsylvania. Four of these five, however, were small states. For the Union to succeed, not only Pennsylvania but also Massachusetts, New York, and Virginia had to come in. In the late winter and spring of 1788 the Antifederalists redoubled their efforts in these states. The champions of the Constitution could brush off many attacks, but one nagging question they could not answer:

V.2: Why had they not included a bill of rights in the Constitution? Why did not the charter of the Republic, like the Declaration of Independence, proclaim the inalienable liberties of the individual?

Narr: "I will now add what I do not like [about the Constitution],"

Thomas Jefferson wrote James Madison from France. "First, the omission of a bill of rights."

After New Hampshire and Virginia had ratified the Constitution, an inspired Alexander Hamilton turned the tide against the Antifederalists who were dominant in his state. The New York convention was persuaded by Hamilton to ratify the plan on July 26. That left two states undecided. North Carolina voted no in August 1788 but changed its mind a year later; Rhode Island straggled into the Union in May 1790. But the demand for a bill of rights proved irresistible.

V.4 (as though giving a campaign speech): James Madison campaigned on a promise to introduce such a bill to Congress. (Not a speech any longer) When I was elected to the House of Representatives, I kept my promise. In March 1789 Congress sent twelve proposed amendments to the states. Two nonessential ones—setting Congressional salaries and going into detail about how many people a Congressman's district should include—were dropped. The other ten—the Bill of Rights largely patterned after the Virginia Declaration of Rights of 1776 primarily penned by George Mason—became part of the Constitution on December 15, 1791.

Narr: These ten amendments are the culmination of the tradition that had originated in the Middle Ages and had been carried on by the English-speaking forebears of the colonists. The amendments completed the Constitution, just as the spire crowns a cathedral. Indeed, when the Constitution is mentioned today, the odds are that the speaker is thinking primarily of this Bill of Rights, along with the "We the People" preamble. These join the Constitution to the Declaration of Independence as the two great American documents proclaiming "the Blessings of Liberty," all thanks to a small assembly of demi-gods.

Getting Rid of Violence against Women: What Will Do the Job

Marcia Pally

I would like to begin by briefly going over the policies recommended to us by the Meese Commission in its recent report. It divides pornography into four categories: violent sex, degrading sex, sex with neither violence nor degradation, and "mere nudity." "Degradation" includes any posture that "depicts women as objects for the sexual satisfaction of men (i.e., depicts women in a decidedly subordinate role with respect to sex, and in general depicts women engaged in practices that would, to most people, be considered humiliating)." The commission's report suggests that all categories except "mere nudity" be prosecuted under obscenity laws, with sex and violence taking the highest priority. It also encourages communities to employ boycotts, pickets, and pressure tactics to protest whatever pornography is left.

In the light of such sentiments, I would like to describe a few of the things that have happened in this country during the pornography debate of the last few years, which had as its highlights the Hudnut case in Indianapolis and the recent Meese Commission Report.

- In the spring of 1986, *Webster's Ninth New Collegiate Dictionary* was removed from classrooms and libraries in a southern school district because it contains definitions of obscene words. A supervisor of English departments there links the dictionary's removal to the climate created by a campaign for a local obscenity law.
- In Denver, antipornography groups have so persistently heckled King Sooper and Safeway markets about the cover art on romance novels that wholesalers have canceled orders from the publisher.
- April 10, 1986, amid much media fanfare, Southland Corporation told all of its 7-Eleven stores around the country to discontinue sales of *Playboy*, *Penthouse*, and *Forum* magazines. A few weeks later, the drugstore chain Rite Aid— which also owns Encore Books—followed suit, along with several other retailers.

- In North Carolina in winter 1986, a judge ruled several R-rated films obscene, including *A Passage to India, Victor Victoria, A Clockwork Orange,* and *Splash.* Over the course of the next few months, a University of North Carolina course in the films of Bertolucci and Federico Fellini was canceled because the professor was afraid someone might lodge an obscenity complaint. Moreover, the paintings of a number of artists were removed from art galleries. North Carolina also passed an obscenity bill that allows the police to close book and video stores and fine merchants for selling pornography *before* the offending material has been judged obscene in court. In other words, a local merchant can be arrested for selling magazines he had no way of knowing were legally obscene. As if that were not enough of a chilling effect, the state of North Carolina and the federal government have formed the first state-federal-local task force on pornography to, as U.S. Attorney Sam Currin put it, "totally shut them down and run them out." FBI agents there have been stopping video shop patrons as they leave stores and asking them what tapes they purchased or rented.

Such events are not restricted to North Carolina. California faces a new law that broadens the definition of obscenity (from material "utterly without redeeming social importance" to that which "lacks significant literary, artistic, political, or scientific value") so that more works may be prosecuted. Abolishing the community standard for obscenity, the law also established one set of criteria for the entire state. Los Angeles cannot have a law more liberal than Bakersfield's.

California also boasts the country's first pornography rock music obscenity case. Jello Biafra, whose group the Dead Kennedys specializes in political satire, has been charged for a sexually explicit poster accompanying the album *Frankenchrist.* Ironically, this is the first of their albums to carry a warning label on the cover to the effect that some people might find the poster "shocking, repulsive or offensive," adding that life can sometimes be that way.

The music industry is having other troubles. Last July, the powerful Wal-Mart chain, which has nine hundred stores in twenty-two states, dropped all rock and roll magazines and some records and tapes because of their "offensive" material. Among the publications listed are *Rolling Stone, Cream,* and *Star Hits;* among the artists whose recordings were removed are comedians Eddie Murphy and Redd Foxx. Other chains have been considering following Wal-Mart's example. As of last August, Randalls in Texas was evaluating forty music industry magazines.

Scuttling schoolbooks and music magazines, film courses and paintings, removing *Playboy* from store shelves, and creating new state obscenity laws are just the beginning. There are likely more

*Passage to India*s to come. Southland representatives said they banned *Playboy, Penthouse,* and *Forum* because testimony at the Meese commission demonstrated "a possible link between porn and crime, violence and child abuse." In fact, the whole antipornography movement—feminist or federal—hangs its hat on the belief that pornography is the cause of rape and the mistreatment of children.

You will notice, by the way, that I mentioned feminist antipornography activists together with other antiobscenity groups. This makes many women uncomfortable. Catherine MacKinnon and Andrea Dworkin, the authors of the antipornography law that was passed in Indianapolis in 1986, have tried strenuously to distinguish their bill from standard obscenity laws. But although there are some philosophical differences, the effect on sexually explicit material would be much the same. First of all, the definition of *pornography* in the Indianapolis law is very broad. It states that pornography is the "sexually explicit subordination of women, graphically depicted, whether in pictures or in words, that also includes one of the following": the law then outlines nine criteria, including presenting women as sexual objects, presenting women in positions that invite penetration, or presenting women being penetrated by objects. I guess this last could mean a finger or a vibrator. I suspect this would be a disappointment to many women.

The second way the Dworkin-MacKinnon bill is similar to standard obscenity codes is the way it sets prosecutions into motion. It permits legal action under four conditions. The first and easiest to put into practice is known as the trafficking provision and operates very much like standard obscenity law. It makes the production, sale, exhibition, and distribution of pornography illegal and permits any woman at any time to bring suit against the shopowner who stocks the material that offends her; she can also sue the author, the photographer, the distributors, etc.

This law was considered so broad and so thoroughly unconstitutional that two judges, one a woman and both Reagan appointees, threw it out. The Supreme Court not only refused to hear arguments on appeal, it unanimously affirmed the lower courts' decisions. There has not been such cohesiveness on the bench since the Alien and Sedition Act.

I am grateful for the efforts of Catherine MacKinnon, Andrea Dworkin, and Edwin Meese to protect women from violence, but it seems pertinent to ask if the pornography-causes-harm theory is correct. Is pornography a significant factor in rape, battery, and incest? Will getting rid of pornography diminish violence against women and children? Or is it merely a progressive patina on old-fashioned sin and morality finger-wagging? After all, the pornography-causes-harm argument makes the banning of books, magazines, rock and roll, and videos seem reasonable to millions of Americans who would laugh at threats of brimstone and hellfire. Is it a "quick fix" that kids us into thinking the solution to abuse is just a matter of banning dirty pictures? Worse, is it a distraction that turns our attention away from the real causes of harm and prevents us from finding solutions?

The pornography-causes-rape argument is easy to understand, easy to sell. It claims that pornography degrades and violates women; men look at it and emulate what they see. So the course of action seems clear: get rid of pornography. The road to victory looks short and direct; it has the lure of "peace in our time."

This argument also has the cachet of feminist tradition. Throughout the seventies, women examined images in all sectors of culture, from television commercials to the films shown in medical school. It was a tool for identifying sexism and exposing its pervasiveness. It makes sense to apply this technique to pornography. But as we do, I think some are confusing the process of examining images for their insights about society with the process of calling those images *sources* or *causes* of social injustice. Feminists who exposed the symbols of sexism fifteen years ago never claimed that taking floor wax commercials off the air would bring us abortion rights or better pay. Or stop rape.

The mass-market pornography industry took off only after World War II. Before the twentieth century, few people save the wealthy elite saw any pornography whatsoever. Yet violence and sexism have been flourishing for thousands of years and nobody needed pornography to show them how to do it. Most of history's rapists, misogynists, and child abusers read nothing at all. And if we look at societies where no pornography is permitted, like Saudi Arabia or Iran, we do not exactly see societies with strong women's rights records. We find instead a great deal of violence against women. If pornography were essential to discrimination against women or to the degradation of women, women would be better off living in Iran than in the United States. So it seems unlikely to me that sexism and rape are directly linked to sexually explicit pictures. It seems unlikely that pornography initiates violence or causes low salaries for women.

It seems more reasonable that violence against women begins with economic discrimination through which men learn to consider women as burdens and with the infantilization of women—either as fragile figurines or hormonal hurricanes—so that men hold women in contempt. It seems more reasonable that violence against women begins with "boy training," which makes aggression a daily project of masculinity, and with childrearing arrangements that leave Mom as the prime—often only—caretaker.

50

It is on Mom that all one's infantile expectations are foisted and all one's earliest disappointments are blamed. Dad comes into the picture only later, as a firm but reasonable force. So we act out our desire for Mom's attention and our rage that she is not always there against all the women in the rest of our lives. Though we all were raised more by Mom than by Dad in infancy, there is an edge of ire men feel about women that women do not feel because, after all, women are "us."

All this shows up in pornography, just as it does in high art, advertising, and fashion. And because pornography is a genre of extremes—schematic, repetitive, ritualistic, fantastic—it exaggerates and distills our psychosexual blueprints. It blows up and illuminates our discomfort with the goo and nakedness of sex, our panic at our arousal and loss of control, and men's lust for and anger at the female figure.

But pornography did not start any of this, and getting rid of pornography will not end it. Pornography may be sexist, as much of it is; it may be racist or violent, as some of it is. But it is silly to call it a cause of sexism, racism, or violence. More important, it is silly to think that banning it will halt the mayhem. I am afraid that the antipornography brouhaha of the last few years is a red herring, luring us away from the sources of sexism and its solutions. I am especially disappointed at the women who have leapt aboard the antipornography bandwagon. Women's rights have progressed in this country because women were able to say and print things that many people believe are not only dangerous but morally degenerate. Women most of all should know the value of a free press.

If we want to halt rape, battery, and incest, feminists and federal commissions would do well to look at the political and economic systems that keep women poor and powerless. We would do well to fight for equal and equivalent pay, nontraditional jobs, a feminist presence in politics, self-defense classes, sex education, better and better-disseminated birth control—the list is all too familiar.

If we want to address the *psychological* fuel behind misogyny, we would do well to look at the family and imbalances in parenting. Feminists and federal commissions would better spend their time not closing pornography parlors but getting Mom out of the house at least half the time and Dad back in. In such a world we would still have pornography where we played out our desires and fears— some of which are not nice—but the pictures and tales we would invent for ourselves might be less sexist.

I would like to take a minute to examine how the Meese commission came to the conclusion that pornography causes violence. Unlike the 1970 presidential commission on pornography that found no causal link, the Meese commission sponsored no research of its own. It held six public hearings and heard testimony mostly from vice squad officers, obscenity prosecutors, representatives of pro-decency organizations, and people who identified themselves as "vic-tims" of pornography. Not a single artist or writer was invited to speak; those who asked to be heard encountered significant resis-tance. Few psychologists or sex educators who do not *a priori* support suppression of pornography were given a forum. (In March 1986, the American Civil Liberties Union issued a thirty-page report on the commission's biased and unprofessional procedures and was forced to sue the commission for illegally withholding public documents. The commission capitulated at the end of April.)

Henry Hudson, district attorney from Arlington County, Virginia, chaired the commission. His tough law-and-order policies closed nearly all "adult" movie theaters and bookstores in the Arling-ton area. "I live to put people in jail," Hudson told *The Washington Post*.

The commission relied on a number of laboratory studies that suggest pornographic images affect attitudes about rape. Many women's antipornography groups rely on these studies as well. But *attitudes*, as even the scientists doing this research will tell you, are notori-ously poor predictors of behavior. People just do not accomplish with any statistical reliability what they say they will. Moreover, we have no idea how long laboratory effects last. What few data we have in-dicate that changes in attitudes are temporary. And no matter what people do in an experimental situation, they know that they are par-ticipating in an experiment, make-believe. No one is really going to get hurt.

Ed Donnerstein, one of the major researchers on this subject, called the commission's conclusions "bizarre." He and other research-ers such as Neil Malamuth found no change in attitudes when men were shown nonviolent sexual images. Donnerstein has been so an-gry at the misuse of his research that he wrote a number of articles (*Psychology Today*, December 1986; *American Behavioral Scientist* 29:5 [1986], pp. 601–18) emphasizing several points. He notes that violent images in *Playboy* have *decreased* over the last ten years and, most important, that antipornography groups continue to ignore the findings that *violence*—nonsexual violence—is what affects the attitudes of his research subjects. In fact, one of his studies (with Linz and Berkowitz) shows that men report the most callous atti-tudes about rape after viewing violent films without sexual content. Conversely, the men who saw erotic films without violence had the most sympathetic attitudes toward women. This finding supports other research (by L. T. Garcia, *The Journal of Sex Research* 22:3 [1986] pp. 378–85) indicating that exposure to sexually explicit mate-rial did not predict much of men's attitudes about women or rape, except that exposure to nonviolent erotica was slightly connected to liberal rather than traditionally restrictive attitudes about women.

Even research that measures the effects of "degrading" pornography is inconclusive. Dolf Zillman, from the Indiana University, found that viewing several hours of "stag" films lowered men's respect for women; Donnerstein, on the other hand, found no change in men's attitudes about rape or loss of sympathy for rape victims.

When the Meese Commission released its findings, several other researchers told *The New York Times* that "violence in the social environment" was more to blame for rape or sexism than depictions of sex. The Society for the Scientific Study of Sex called the commission's conclusions "incomplete and inadequate" and a danger to future sex research. Just last May, the Institute of Criminal Justice in Copenhagen reported that in European countries where restrictions on pornography have been lifted, the incidence of rape over the last ten to twenty years has declined or remained constant. Neither the Canadian nor the British studies of pornography found it to be the cause of sexual violence.

On a more individual or personal note, Commissioners Dr. Judith Becker and Ellen Levine were so appalled by the way their colleagues handled social science data that they issued a dissenting report. Lambasting the commission for a "paucity of certain types of testimony including dissenting expert opinion," they concluded, "No self-respecting investigator would accept the conclusions based on such a study." They rejected the commission's finding that most pornography sold in the United States is "degrading" and could lead to violence, and they rejected several law enforcement recommendations (including mandatory prison sentences for certain violations of obscenity law). Dr. Becker, director of the Sexual Behavior Clinic at New York State Psychiatric Institute, added, "I've been working with sex offenders for 10 years and have reviewed the scientific literature and I don't think a causal link exists between porn and sex crimes."

I would like to consider some other arguments of the pornography-causes-harm doctrine. Some statistics show that convicted rapists are guilty of acts pictured in pornography. Certainly gruesome things have been done to women for centuries without *Hustler*'s help. Still other data demonstrate that communities with more pornography report more rapes. Yet higher incidences of rape are also found in areas with strong sales of any men's magazines, such as *Field & Stream*.

But what about women's personal experiences? Women say their boyfriends or husbands get ideas from pornography and force them to do what the photographs depict. But the problem is not kama sutra positions. The problem is *force*—economic, psychological, and physical. It is not only profligate to tell women that their problems at home begin with pornography, it is dangerous. Such claims delude and mislead women, leaving them farther from improving the conditions of their lives. I can think of few greater treacheries.

What about the rapists and wife batterers who say they learned their crimes from pornography? It is a clever ploy. Just look at who gets off the hook: First it was the devil that made them do it; now it is Miss Jones. And something is not quite right about the proposition that men rape because they learned—from pornography—that it is okay or that women like it.

One thing feminism accomplished was the redefinition of rape from a sexual act to a violent one. But I suspect it was always clear to the rapist facing his terrified victim that she did not "want it." Men rape because it hurts, and they do it to hurt us. If we want to deal with rape, we ought to deal with *why* men rape women. What is going on in "real life" that makes men want to inflict so much pain?

There is still a nagging question: why does the antipornography argument feel so right? Why does it seem persuasive to so many men and women? To begin with, it offers the appeal of activism. Since pornography is visible, easy to identify, and already illicit, one can organize against it relatively easily. Witness the renown that Women against Pornography has achieved in just five or six years. The participants feel that they are doing something to improve women's lot, and we all need to feel effective.

Psychologist Paula Webster suggests that something else is going on. She believes the antipornography argument feels right because it carries "the voice of mom." And she may have a point. Most of us have grown up with the idea that sex is "icky"; most women have grown up with the assurance that men are dangerous. We have heard it indirectly or we have heard it point blank, but we have heard it all our lives.

As adults, most of us manage "to get our own." But the old lessons remain embedded in our imaginations and at the core of our emotions. So when we are told that pornography is disgusting and makes men dangerous, it "clicks." When we hear—in adult language and political terminology—things we absorbed when we were little, it sounds infallible. Already suspicious of sex, we are ready to call sex the culprit.

There is a great deal of violence done to women—the FBI reports that a woman is beaten every eighteen seconds and raped every few minutes. But rage and violence are the core of the problem, not sexually explicit images. And we must get at the core, using our time and resources shrewdly. In the past few years, feminists and the media have spent a great deal of money on the pornography debate.

Yet last year New York Women against Rape nearly closed for lack of funds. It still operates month to month. And the government that funded the Meese Commission withheld allocations earmarked for battered women's shelters because they were ostensibly "antifamily." No one is going to convince me that a government that has rolled back affirmative action, fought against comparable worth, and stripped hundreds of programs that benefit women and children opposes pornography because it is dangerous to those very same women and children.

We cannot afford to be duped—either by a duplicitous government or by what "feels right." Rape, battery, and discrimination thrived for centuries without pornography. If we get rid of it, we will still be left with rape, battery, and discrimination. Would that the solution to women's problems—or simply to rape—were merely a matter of eliminating pornography. Would that it were so single-issue, or so easy.

There is a second reason to be skeptical of the sex-is-disgusting/men-are-dangerous echo. It is protective, defensive, and meant to shield women from harm. But although women must protect themselves with political, economic, and physical clout, we cannot be only defensive. We cannot live our lives in fear. Eighty years ago, when conditions for women were far less felicitous than today, Emma Goldman understood that. Women have to develop their appetites and find out what it feels like to spend time and money on sex, and we cannot wait till after the revolution.

No one is in the mood to flirt or seduce and have adventures when she is thoroughly scared. Fear paralyzes. The antipornography movement, focusing on danger rather than on its remedies, paralyzes. It teaches fear.

Women cannot afford to build a movement—or mind a government—that tells us sex, or pictures and fantasies about sex, are so frightening that we give them up. We cannot scurry away from passion or pictures of passion hoping that if we stay away from them altogether we will be safe. We cannot be persuaded into thinking that sex is sexist. If we do, we will end up denying ourselves the replenishment and ego boost that sex brings in an exchange for bogus safety or security—as though such a denial would even provide them. We owe ourselves more than that. We need to pursue not only protection but power and pleasure. Women do deserve it.

Beyond the relationship of images to their audience lies the issue of images and the actors and models who make them. Linda Marchiano—who was known as Linda Lovelace—wrote a book, *Ordeal*, about how she was held against her will, beaten, and forced to perform the acts we see in one of pornography's biggest hits, *Deep Throat*. Antipornography feminists claim that thousands of women are coerced and raped in the pornography industry and that their rapes are sold as pornographic entertainment.

First, I think it is important to say perhaps the obvious: in theater and film, everything that looks violent is not painful to the actors. As anyone who has ever been in a school play knows, what looks horrid to the audience may be just a matter of lighting and ketchup. But Linda Marchiano is not talking about illusion; she is talking about real violence. For all of us concerned about rape and battery, working conditions in the sex industry are of genuine concern.

Candida Royalle was a pornography actress for many years and is now head of Femme Productions, making her own pornographic videotapes. I would like to give you her description of the pornography industry; it accords with what several other women have told me. Candida reminded me that pornography is a highly competitive field; producers are turning people away, not forcing them to stay. But she also said that, although she never came across it, there undoubtedly was sexual abuse in the industry, because there is sexual abuse of women in every job.

So what should we do about instances of kidnapping, coercion, or rape in pornography settings? The problem here, to my mind, is not pornography any more than sexual abuse in an insurance office means that the problem is insurance. The problem is that the laws against violence are rarely enforced in the sex industry and that police treat complaints so cavalierly that women—and men—in the industry do not bother to file them.

It seems, then, that if feminists and federal commissioners want to get rid of violence in the sex industry, we have to work on getting antiviolence laws enforced in pornography and prostitution settings. And we have to work on getting women—including women in the sex industries—treated with respect in the precincts and in the courts. If we destroy photographs of a rape, we are still left with the rape when the photos are burned. But if we diminish the violence there will not be any pictures of it to be sold as pornography.

A second kind of coercion connected with the sex industries is economic—where women and men, boys and girls, are forced into modeling or prostitution because it is the best-paying job around. If we close the pornography industry, we wipe out a source of income that is crucial to many people no matter how dismaying it may be to some of us, and yet we provide no alternatives. If we drive the pornography industry underground, we make those jobs more dangerous because everything is more violent and hazardous on the black market. At every pornography panel I have attended over the past few years, women from the sex industry have stood up and angrily pointed this fact out.

Would it not be more effective to work on job training for the teenagers, men, and women in the sex industry, if they want it? Would it not make more sense to ask them what they want? It may take longer than driving pornography underground, but ridding ourselves of pornography reduces options. Education and job opportunities increase them. And if we were really serious about ensuring the safety of women and men in the sex industry, we would make those industries completely legitimate: the more legitimate, the more accountable to the law.

Most important, we need to hear from sex industry workers, to listen to what they need, to how they would like to improve their work conditions. And we need to support their organizations, like the U.S. Prostitutes Collective, COYOTE (Cast Off Your Old Tired Ethics), PUMA (Prostitutes Union of Massachusetts), the California Prostitutes Education Project, and the International Committee for Prostitutes' Rights.

Pornography
and the First Amendment

J. Michael Loomis

The English language must be a terribly difficult language for a foreigner to use and understand. We have strayed a great distance from Old English. So many words have unique and double meanings and are dependent upon their contexts. We use euphemisms in everyday conversations, words that one can understand only if one has heard them before.

Unfortunately, we frequently take advantage of certain phrases and terms of art. For instance, when we talk about "xeroxing a copy," we generally mean making a photocopy. *Xerox* is a trademark that belongs to a corporation. Or, when we refer to a "frisbee" we generally mean any round plastic saucer designed to be thrown by kids. In truth, that name is a registered trademark of a corporation. But, in those instances we do not care. It does not make any real difference to the general public, since there usually is no misunderstanding.

Now, this misfortune can also befall expressions that have more import. When a word is used to capture a specific meaning and it is substituted interchangeably with another, we create confusion. *Pornography* and *obscenity* are two such words. *Pornography* is a term that applies to the general category of "sexually explicit materials." There are no laws against pornography, per se. *Obscenity* is a term that applies to a difficult-to-define area, an area within the realm of pornography. Not all pornography is obscene. "Semantics!" you say? *Obscenity* is a legal expression; it is a term of art, just as "tort," "probate," "administration," and "eminent domain" are words and phrases that give particular meaning to narrow legal concepts.

There are laws against the distribution and exhibition of obscene matter at both the federal and state levels. Every state except Alaska has enacted such legislation. Most, but not all, use the definition of obscenity that was set out by the United States Supreme Court in *Miller* v. *California* (1973).

The test employs a three-part inquiry; whether

(1) the average person, applying contemporary community standards, finds that the dominant theme of the matter or performance, taken as a whole, appeals to a prurient interest in sex;
(2) the matter or performance depicts or describes, in a patently offensive way, sexual conduct; *and*
(3) the matter or performance, taken as a whole, lacks serious literary, artistic, political, or scientific value.

As you can see, one of these three parts deals with community standards.

A state, by virtue of its legislative power, has broad authority to create criminal offenses in order to protect and promote the public welfare and preserve individual freedom and safety. That such authority includes the right to enact legislation against obscenity has been endorsed time and again by the United States Supreme Court.

This raises some interesting questions, questions that were enumerated very clearly in a recent article in *Time* magazine entitled "Sex Busters" (July 21, 1986). The questions asked were the following: "Is morality a question of individual rights? What is the role of the state in enforcing the morality of its citizenry? How far should the government go in regulating private conduct? Should the state play an active role in nurturing values deemed worthy by the community?" By and large these questions are posing essentially the same inquiry: "Where do we draw the line?"

Many would oppose the drawing of any line. But nearly every law legislates morality in setting some standard for its citizens, and every citizen must ultimately make the moral decision to obey or disobey. As we are a government of the people, for the people, and by the people, we also must remember that a majority favors regulation of obscene matter. *U.S.* v. *Miller* was never challenged by Congress. I infer that this is the result of an agreement among citizens that private morals are private, but public morals are the business of the entire community; that what you do in the privacy of your own home is your own business, but that your privacy right does not extend to the marketplace.

It is interesting that the artwork on the cover of the *Time* magazine I mentioned earlier contained such a cynical caricature. It depicted three wide-eyed men with a look of disgust on their faces. One held a Bible; a second held a pair of rather large scissors; and the third wore a robe and carried a gavel. By the way, the man with the scissors is carrying a stamp which is easily read: "Censorship."

The word *censor* is derived from a term used to describe Roman officers who acted as census takers, assessors and reviewers of public morals and conduct. Presumably enforcement was arbitrary and selective. Today, *censor* or *censure* has come to mean pre-emptive action. It is commonly associated with the phrase "prior restraint," that is, prohibition of a publication before it is published. To imply or claim that by enacting laws against obscenity, a government is imposing a form of censorship is, simply put, a mistake!

To make such an argument is to presume that obscene materials rise to the level of protection afforded by the First Amendment. Until the United States Supreme Court reverses itself, the exceptions to First Amendment materials will continue to disqualify some aspects of expression from constitutional coverage.

You cannot yell "Fire!" in a crowded theatre; you cannot utter libelous and slanderous untruths; you cannot publish information relative to the national security; you cannot provoke someone to the level of angry action; and you cannot distribute or exhibit obscene material.

Enforcement of laws against obscenity occurs after the fact. The offense has already been committed before charges are initiated by the state. There is no pre-emptive action, since a determination of the obscenity of a particular item is not made before the offense.

An arrest warrant is issued in all obscenity cases only after probable cause is found. Probable cause is determined by a neutral and detached magistrate. It is also reviewed at the initial hearing and it is evaluated a third time when someone requests an adversary hearing. More to the point, a final determination is made by a jury of one's peers applying community standards about whether the questioned matter is obscene. Censorship, as an argument against the enforcement of obscenity legislation, fails of its own merits.

At the same time, understanding that laws are enacted to prevent or deter a specific type of conduct, I would agree that enforcing the obscenity laws "chills" the commercial dissemination of obscene matter, at least insofar as it deters violators of the law. However, it strikes me that this is the desired effect, the legislative intent. It also is apparent to me that judicial pronouncements against a "chilling effect" in certain laws and their enforcement apply only to material that receives First Amendment protection. Obscenity does not. Therefore, there are no proscriptions against the creation of a chilling effect on the dissemination of obscene matter.

The work of the Indiana Civil Liberties Union, the American Civil Liberties Union, and other civil liberties groups is valuable and important. Their efforts make everyone involved in legal battles better lawyers; they help sharpen the issues. However, I am amused at times by the rhetoric employed to taint enforcement of existing law. I do not think the ICLU and ACLU have a corner on the market for protecting individual rights and liberties. Every attorney in the state of Indiana must take an oath upon admission to the bar. This oath begins with the words, "I do solemnly swear or affirm that I will support the Constitution of the United States and the Constitution of the State of Indiana." As a deputy prosecutor, I had to take a second oath that contained essentially the same vow, as well as a promise to fully and faithfully enforce the laws of the state.

The Indianapolis ordinance is frequently mentioned in discussions about obscenity and the law. However, this measure is to be distinguished from state law, which forms the basis of prosecution against obscenity. Generally, women's groups have, in the last several years, attempted to persuade legislatures to adopt laws that would make trafficking in pornography a form of discrimination against women. This notion is actually a civil rights approach, defining pornography in terms of the sexual subordination, abuse, and degradation of women. It is based upon the premise that pornography causes discrimination, aggression, and violence against women.

On June 15, 1984, the City-County Council of Indianapolis enacted such a civil rights law. That ordinance made it against the law to traffic in pornography, to coerce another into a pornographic performance, or to force another into sexual acts as a result of pornography. This approach, again, is to be distinguished from state law, which uses the "Miller" test of obscenity.

Under the Indianapolis ordinance, anyone claiming to be aggrieved by pornography would have the authority to file a lawsuit against the person engaging in the discriminatory practice, such as the maker, seller, exhibitor, or distributor of pornography.

In the case of trafficking in pornography, any woman could file a complaint (representing the "class" of women generally) against subordination of women.

The constitutionality of the ordinance was subsequently attacked after its passage by the City-County Council. It was held unconstitutional in *American Booksellers Association* v. *Hudnut*, 598 F. Supp. (S.D. Ind. 1984).

The United States Supreme Court found that the ordinance regulated speech that was entitled to First Amendment protection. The court then sought to determine whether "the state's interest in protecting women from the humiliation and degradation which came from being depicted in a sexually subordinate context is so compelling as to warrant the regulation of otherwise free speech to accomplish the end."

The court concluded that it was not and explained that women are capable of protecting themselves from being harmed by pornography, saying that "to deny free speech in order to engineer social change in the name of accomplishing a greater good for one sector of our society erodes the freedom of all."

The United States Court of Appeals for the Seventh Circuit agreed with the district court, indicating that the ordinance affected speech that did not fall within the exceptions I mentioned earlier, such as libel, fighting words, or obscenity.

The Seventh Circuit Court did, however, accept the basic premise that pornography subordinates and degrades women. The court said, "Pornography is central in creating and maintaining sex as a basis of discrimination. Pornography is a systematic practice of exploitation and sex which differentially harms women. The bigotry and contempt it produces, with the acts of aggression it fosters, harms women's opportunities for equality and rights."

Remember, if you will, my remarks regarding the distinction between the terms *obscenity* and *pornography*.

It was, undoubtedly, the failure of the City-County Council to target an area of unprotected speech that led to the demise of the ordinance. You cannot legally attack the general notion of pornography without complying with strict constitutional standards interpreted in conjunction with the First Amendment.

The city of Indianapolis appealed to the United States Supreme Court and on February 24, 1986, the court summarily affirmed the judgment of the Court of Appeals.

There is a narrow school of thought that subscribes to the notion that artistic expression and enforcement of obscenity laws are incompatible. To those persons I say, the continuing viability of artistic expression is not threatened. There are several safeguards involved in prosecuting obscenity violations, safeguards that protect cultural freedom. First of all, obscenity laws are narrow by definition. The only definition that has been found constitutionally sound is that which complies with the Miller test. Thus pornography is not the basis for a criminally prosecutable offense (unless, of course, it involves minors). Second, the application of the Miller test takes place in an open courtroom, with a gallery and press in attendance. Third, application of the definition of obscenity is decided by a jury. Fourth, the matter prosecuted must involve the depiction of sexual conduct. Fifth, that depiction must offend contemporary community standards. Finally, the subject matter must involve material that lacks serious literary, artistic, political, or scientific value.

The legal definition of *obscenity* is an instruction that a jury is entitled to read and must follow. Artistic value is a proper and effective defense if the jury is so convinced.

The objective of any prosecutor, I think, is to enforce the law fully, aggressively, and consistently with an attitude of fairness. At the same time, we must strive to be cognizant and tolerant of individual liberties and rights. Striking a balance between the two is not always easy; in fact, it is sometimes unpopular. The controversy, in at least this instance, goes far beyond the mere enforcement of a certain category of offenses.

Religious Freedom
and the Constitution

Dean M. Kelley

The contention that has just surfaced judicially in Alabama, that failure to mention religion in the course of public school classroom education constitutes the establishment of another religion, secular humanism, is really one of the more remarkable exercises of logic in the judicial realm—one that I first encountered about twenty years ago at the behest of a good friend of mine, Bill Ball, who is a Catholic attorney in Harrisburg, Pennsylvania. I thought it was a little strained at the time, and I still do. But it has now received judicial recognition, and I suppose we will have to deal with it in various ways.

First let me say that I feel fortunate to be on the same platform with Dr. Hitchcock. Since he reviewed my first book favorably, he can't be all bad. In fact I have respected him for his work and his writings ever since. And I think he has raised a significant problem in our society—is neutrality a myth, an impossible ideal? It is perhaps too early to tell. We have only been at this for a couple of hundred years and, in the course of history, that is not a very long time.

Our forebears who framed the fundamental law upon which the nation rests, the framers of the Constitution, tried a very radical and revolutionary institutional invention. They staked their lives and their fortunes and their sacred honor on an idea that had not been tried elsewhere: that the civil covenant could be divorced from the religious covenant. That is, a society could be based upon something other than a shared and common religious faith to which everyone was supposed to adhere. That had been the pattern, more or less, in the European experience, and, for a time, it was rather strenuously carried out to the degree that those persons who did not conform to the prevailing religious faith (or pretend to) were executed or at least exiled. Later, in the more effete years of European history, when a little greater diversity occurred thanks to the Protestant Reformation, there were small Protestant nation-states neighboring similar Catholic states. And then various varieties of Protestantism emerged—

Lutheran, Calvinist, etc. So the principle grew up that "whoever rules, his religion will prevail." If a ruling prince were Catholic, everybody was supposed to be Catholic; if he was succeeded suddenly by a Protestant, everybody was supposed to become Protestant. If that seems ridiculous, one can recall that that is exactly what happened in England when Mary was succeeded by Elizabeth I. There were other successions there, similarly sudden, when the rules of the game suddenly changed, and anyone who could not make the shift was expected at least to keep quiet and not cause scandal by overt non-conformity. And, if they could not do that, they were to move to a realm that would be more receptive to their peculiar ideas—if one could be found. That tradition of "endure or emigrate" was what prevailed in Europe under the pattern of territorialism. That is, religion matched the territory ruled by a given prince, whose religion was to prevail in that territory.

But our forebears were not satisfied with that arrangement. They came to this country to try another one. The founders initiated this great adventure of seeing if a nation could work in which the people did not have to belong to one favored established religion. They thought that they would try the vision of Roger Williams, who wrote the famed Ship Metaphor, starting out "there goes many a ship to sea" in which different religions are to be found among the passengers, but the ship can still proceed upon its voyage and reach its destination if they are not obliged to go to the ship's prayers. As long as they behave themselves properly and do not cause disruption of the ship's sailing, it does not matter much what their particular religions may be. Roger Williams actually tried that in the colony he founded, Rhode Island; William Penn tried something similar in Pennsylvania. So the new arrangement was not totally without precedent. But the founders of this country decided that they would try it on a national scale, and they wrote it into the First Amendment, stating, "Congress shall make no law respecting an establishment of religion or prohibiting the free exercise thereof." And the Supreme Court has been trying for many years to spell out what those two countervailing clauses mean. Ideally they should be the obverse and the reverse of one coin of religious freedom, but sometimes they seem to be in conflict.

It is true that most of the church-state jurisprudence in this country has emerged since 1940 and 1948, when the Supreme Court announced that the religion clauses of the First Amendment applied not just to Congress but through the Fourteenth Amendment also to the states. And since most of the religious turmoil in the country was at a state or local level, this kind of internecine conflict over religious issues began to boil up to the Supreme Court level. Although I agree, in general, with most of what the Supreme Court

64

has said on that subject, there are a few instances where I think it has reached somewhat ridiculous extremes. We do not need to go into what all those are at present; but I think in the particular area of school prayer we have seen some excesses, perhaps, brought about by local courts trying to follow out consistently what they thought the Supreme Court was trying to say.

The court has had a lot of school prayer cases before it and, perhaps, the end is not yet here—or at least it is moving in a different direction. I sometimes wonder why the good justices of the Supreme Court choose to hear the cases they do choose. Some of them would strike me as being *de minimis* (that means trifling), and I know that they have declined to hear some cases appealed to them that I consider far more crucial, far more important for freedom of religion. But, at any rate, they seem to like these school prayer cases because they have certainly worked them over a good deal. And, as a result, the opinion has been heard in the land that the court is striving for an impossible ideal of governmental neutrality among different religions and between religion and lack of religion.

I think there are other dynamics at work that we may be able to point to later on, but it is certainly true that as a result of some of the court's decisions and their oversimplification, many public school educators have steered away from anything having to do with religion because it might prove controversial. That has led to, perhaps, a greater neglect of religion in public school education than the Constitution or the Supreme Court requires. I will return to that thought in a moment.

I think this distress about whether neutrality is possible is typical of a set of two-value contrasts that have emerged in this field of late, views that somehow the universe is dichotomized in two parts and only two. There is a set of cases having to do with the teaching of evolution and whether equal time should be given for what is euphemistically called "creation science." The logic of creation science has been to assert that if there is anything that shows that the generally accepted view of evolution is not true, then that automatically must prove that creation is true, overlooking an infinite range of other possibilities that may exist in addition to those two. Similarly, in the Alabama case, two-valued logic has prevailed: that if there is no mention of religion, at least none of a sort expected by and demanded by the plaintiffs, the only other possibility is that there must be an establishment of another religion of secular humanism. Here, too, there is an infinite range of other possibilities in between.

A further kind of instance of the two-valued universe is that if there is no mention of religion, then, in the words of my friend Richard John Newhaus in his recent book (which is much admired by the administration) entitled *The Naked Public Square*, the public square is naked of emblems of the faith of the people that bind the nation together. Therefore, other and possibly demonic faiths will move into the naked public square and take the place of the true faiths of the religious public.

As I intimated at the beginning, it may be that it is a little too early to tell whether the founders' experiment is really going to work. It may be that a nation cannot survive that does not have state-sponsored emblems and practices and rites of the predominant religion implanted in the public square and promulgated in the public institutions such as public schools. I do not, myself, believe that. I think that there are many possibilities in the middle that have been overlooked. I think neutrality is an ideal to be approximated, and it will never be perfectly achieved; but I would hate to see us try the other possibility of a state that seeks to be *unneutral* in matters of religion. We had a lot of that for many centuries, and it was unsatisfactory to our forebears who came here to try something else. So I would hate to see us abandon that experiment at this stage and say that there is no option left to us but to go back to the territorialism of Europe, which is exactly what would happen if state-sponsored school prayer were established as proposed by our esteemed president in his sponsored amendment that failed passage in the Republican-controlled Senate by eleven votes a couple of years ago. It was rather blandly asserted that, of course, *somebody* has to pick the prayer. The people would be responsible for carrying on the schools, and the remedy for any of those who did not like it would be *excusal*.

Now I have been active for twenty years in the efforts to defeat amendments that would reverse the Supreme Court's decision outlawing state-sponsored prayer in public schools. There have been seven such attempts, each one of which has been defeated by the opposition of the main religious bodies of this nation, who feel that state-sponsored school prayer would be the prayer satisfactory to the majority, that it would therefore be unjust to members of minority faiths or no faiths. They also believe that it is unwise because it would be a return to the European pattern, which is that those who cannot profess the prevailing religion of the sovereign (in this country that of the majority of the people) have two choices: either to endure in silence or to emigrate—that is, nonconforming students can ask to be excused and go out of the classroom, emigrate temporarily until the prayer is over and then they can come back in—which puts them in a terribly distressing situation of nonconformity, of making a spectacle of themselves. Each one of these seven attempts to amend the Constitution has foundered on two conundrums: Whose prayer will it be? and How can it be made voluntary? Because those questions could not be solved, Congress has been unwilling to give a two-thirds majority to any such proposal, and I think the tide has peaked and has begun to ebb after the Senate's failing to pass such an amendment a couple of years ago when the president's party had a majority.

The third point about school prayer is that it is unnecessary, because people can pray at any time and at any place. In fact, it is a little mystifying to find "Bible-believing Christians," at least so self-described, seeking to reinstitute state-sponsored school prayer when, if I remember rightly, in the Sermon on the Mount the Lord Jesus Christ says, "And when you pray you must not be like the hypocrites for they love to stand and pray in the synagogues and at the street corners that they may be seen by men. Truly, I say to you, they have their reward. But when you pray go into your room and shut the door and pray to your Father who is in secret, and your Father who sees in secret will reward you." Now, that seems to me to express a different approach to prayer than to have a state-prescribed prayer introduced, scheduled for oral-collective appropriation in a class-room where children are gathered by force of law for essentially non-religious purposes. (I may be giving the whole thing away by saying "essentially nonreligious purposes," but I will get to that in my con-clusion.) They are drawn there not because they belong to the same religious body, but because they live in the same geographic neigh-borhood. That does not constitute a worshipping congregation, as I have understood it; it constitutes a public school classroom. Now the problem is whether that public school classroom with its geo-graphical selection of participants should be transformed by legisla-tive fiat into a worshipping congregation, even for a few minutes. That idea poses a different understanding of prayer from mine and a different one I think from that reflected in the New Testament.

But the idea, in conclusion, that the elimination of state-sponsored devotions in the classroom thereby establishes another re-ligion of secular humanism is a little strained to my way of thinking, because secular humanism, while it may describe a syndrome of atti-tudes, does not constitute a religion. It may constitute a bundle of philosophies but, as far as I know, if you wanted to join the secular humanist religion, I do not know where you would go to do it. I do not know that there is a church devoted to that on the corner any-where or a clergy trained for the purpose of serving it, or a congrega-tion gathered together under that aegis. So for those reasons and others, I think to call it a religion in and of itself is a strange use of words.

The Supreme Court, in striving to approximate the ideal of gov-ernmental neutrality toward religion and therefore eliminating state-sponsored devotions in public school classrooms, has not thereby exiled God or removed all mention of religion. What they have said indicates that study of the Bible or of religion when presented objectively as part of the secular program of education may be effected consistently with the First Amendment. In other words, the court is suggesting that the proper role for a school, oddly enough, is *teaching*, not playing church. And the way to introduce an understanding of religion to students is to *teach* about it in an objective way, if possible; and objectivity, like neutrality, is not a perfect state but an ideal to be approximated. And one has only to ask oneself whether one wants the government to approximate nonobjectivity or nonneutrality to see the error of that course. But the fault is not with the court or the law; the fault is with us and with the public schools based in our communities that have failed to follow this advice, grossly failing to follow it in just such instances as were mentioned in the Alabama textbook case because it might prove controversial. We, the consuming public who support the public schools, have not insisted that they do that. Instead we have been drawn astray by people who want to amend the Constitution to get the public schools back in the devotion business instead of insisting that they teach about religion in some kind of sensible, objective way.

So, instead of railing against the Supreme Court, I think we ought to work more constructively with our own public schools to encourage them to pursue the path left wide open before them by the court itself.

The First Amendment:
The Chimera of Neutrality

James Hitchcock

Church-state issues, arising mostly under the First Amendment to the Constitution, are constantly in the news in our time. It probably would have seemed odd to our ancestors that constitutional questions, some of which hinge on technical and esoteric points, could arouse as much public interest and passion as they do. And, in fact, there are few other countries in the world that have constitutional systems quite like ours. No other country seems to have an institution quite like our Supreme Court, and although our system is supposed to insulate these matters from too great public pressure, at the same time, it tends also to create public issues and keep them alive. Almost all really significant cases involving the interpretation of the First Amendment and the role of religion have occurred in the last forty years, and I think that is worth bearing in mind when people argue that the original intention of the Founding Fathers has been changed or thwarted in some fashion. It has only been since World War II that the Supreme Court has interested itself in any significant and continuing fashion in most of these issues.

There are no systematic studies that I know of, but the evidence suggests that before World War II, and even for a good while afterwards in many places, religion was present in the public schools in all sorts of ways, and people seldom objected. The Bible was read in the public schools, prayers were said daily, sometimes the teachers were clergy, there were graduation ceremonies with heavily religious overtones, teachers in the classroom would invoke the authority of Scripture or of God as a basis for morality, etc. Only in about the last forty years has a systematic attempt been made to insist that these arrangements do, in fact, violate the First Amendment.

By and large, the Supreme Court has been receptive to that argument, so that in the last twenty-five years the Supreme Court has said that there may be no required public prayer in schools; nor may a teacher assign a student to lead a prayer that would have the effect of giving it official sanction; nor may there be an officially required minute of silence at the beginning of the school day, which the Supreme Court a few years ago construed as being a covert attempt to smuggle in official prayer; nor may the state require the posting of the Ten Commandments in every classroom—there are a number of cases of this kind. The list goes on and on. In general, the Supreme Court has made it very clear that no direct and, in certain cases, no indirect expression of religious belief may be present in the public schools in any way that smacks of official approval or official sanction.

The series of Supreme Court decisions that have come down in the last twenty-five years rests upon an assumption that the schools should be neutral. The standard argument has been that the public schools exist to serve everybody, and there are very few communities that are totally homogeneous in religion. We are more heterogeneous now than ever before in terms of religious makeup. There is even one state in the Union that is said not to have a Christian majority, and that is Hawaii. Whereas at one time there were almost no Muslims or Hindus in the United States, as a result of immigration there are now a fair number of them in some places. In addition, of course, there are people who profess no religion at all, unbelievers or agnostics. So the standard argument is that the schools cannot support or cater to religion in any fashion because to do so would be unfair to those who do not fit in. No matter how vague or how general the attempt has been to mandate prayer or a moment of silence, the court has said that such an action is a violation of the Separation Clause of the Constitution.

The question then is this: Is it possible to achieve neutrality, or is this rather rigorous exclusion of religious expression itself sending a negative message? My basic position is the latter, that when the court says, for example, that the state of Kentucky may not require the posting of the Ten Commandments in every classroom, it is sending out an unfortunate message—a message that seems to imply a mistrust of religion, even to some degree hostility toward religion. That message seems unavoidable whatever the intention of the court may have been.

Neutrality, of course, must be neutrality not only among various religions, but, as the court continually points out, also between belief and unbelief. It can be persuasively argued that the purpose of the First Amendment was simply to prevent favoritism from being shown to one church in preference to others, to forbid, for example, the establishment of the Episcopal Church, at the expense of other churches. But it was not the intention of the First Amendment to say that religion and lack of religion are on an equal footing. The modern view is that they should be, that there should be neutrality as regards belief and unbelief. Once again this is the crux of the matter: Is such a neutrality possible, or is a mandated silence with regard to religion itself a message? While the courts have been prohibiting or restricting the explicit expression of religious beliefs in public school classrooms, they have been broadening the scope of free speech. If, for example, a teacher in the public schools were to express controversial political opinions, or were to express a controversial opinion on homosexuality, and such a teacher were fired, the courts might well construe this action as a violation of free speech and order that the teacher be reinstated. There have been cases along this line. If, on the other hand, the teacher were accused of proselytizing for his or her view in the classroom and the teacher were fired, the court would be likely to take the opposite position. This is not neutrality but rather a kind of discrimination against religion.

In 1987, a decision was handed down in Alabama by a federal district judge ruling that the public schools of the state of Alabama have established the religion of secular humanism and thus are in violation of the First Amendment. He ordered the removal of a number of textbooks from the classroom on the grounds that they embody a secular humanist bias. I was a witness for the plaintiffs in that case, the plaintiffs being those who sued the Alabama State Board of Education claiming a secular humanist bias. I was not directly involved with evaluating the textbooks. The contention of the plaintiffs, who are parents and teachers in the Alabama Public School System, is that since the First Amendment is deemed to prohibit all expression of religious belief or all favoritism toward religious belief in the public schools, this interpretation must apply not only to those religions that are explicitly theistic—those that affirm belief in God—but also to religion in general. One of the issues in the case, then, is whether there can be a religion that does not involve belief in God. The common-sense definition of *religion* includes believing in God; but philosophers of religion, sociologists of religion, even a number of theologians define religion much more broadly. The great Protestant theologian Paul Tillich defined religion as "ultimate concern." Most people who study religion as a social reality argue that there can be a religion that does not involve belief in God. The second stage of the argument, then, is that theism, that is, explicit belief in God, has been excluded from the Alabama Public School System and that this constitutes favoritism toward the religion of secular humanism.

Secular humanism has been defined in various ways. I define it myself in pragmatic terms as "living as though there is no God." It is a view of reality that says the here-and-now alone is real and is all we can know. God's existence, if there is a God, has no real bearing on society as we live in it. For all practical purposes human beings are autonomous, are not under any kind of divine plan or divine providence. Secular humanists argue quite vehemently that religion, in the sense of believing in God, is a purely private matter that ought not to have any significant public expression.

There are a number of people who over the years have defined themselves as humanists, sometimes as secular humanists. This term is not something that has been invented by feverish imaginations, as the media would lead you to think. In addition, some of the people who identify themselves as humanists or secular humanists have also insisted quite vigorously that what they profess is indeed a religion. The very influential American philosopher John Dewey is one example. For the purposes of this case, however, the humanists in question tended to deny that it is a religion.

The final stage of the argument, then, was that the textbooks in use in the Alabama public schools reflect this secular humanist bias and amount, therefore, to a form of discrimination against theists. Broadly speaking, two types of evidence were presented. One was absence of important and necessary information about religion. In many history and social studies textbooks, the role of religion in the history of American life has been systematically excluded, minimized, or ignored. Virtually no one, to my knowledge, now denies that lack. There have been several studies that support that contention— for example, stories about the first Thanksgiving that do not mention that the Pilgrims were thanking God, but simply say that they were giving thanks to the Indians. In discussing the Civil Rights movement in the South, the books mention Martin Luther King but not the fact that he was a Baptist minister or that the churches played a major role in the movement. These are examples of the way in which religion has been systematically bleached-out.

The second form of evidence has to do with moral belief in textbooks and, rather surprisingly, includes textbooks in home economics. If you think home economics is mostly a matter of cooking and sewing, as I did, you are in for a surprise when you discover that home economics now deals with all sorts of sensitive moral issues. A bias comes through in many textbooks against the notion of an absolute morality and in favor of a relativist morality, a message given to students in numerous ways: you are the ultimate judge of right and wrong; no one else can tell you what is right and wrong; you decide for yourself what is right and wrong. There is an implication that those—e.g., parents, clergy—who think they know absolute truth are mistaken and that perhaps to claim such knowledge is somewhat dangerous.

The judge has accepted the argument of the plaintiffs: he has ruled that, indeed, the religion of secular humanism is established in the public schools of Alabama and that certain textbooks must, therefore, no longer be used after this year. The case is under appeal and, undoubtedly, will go eventually to the Supreme Court.

There are broad implications in this case in terms of the chimera of neutrality, because the plaintiffs are arguing that the public schools have not achieved such neutrality. Instead, they discriminate against certain beliefs. If children take seriously what they are taught in the public schools, they find the religion of their parents and their churches undermined. If the Supreme Court should uphold this decision, we would have to go back and rethink the very rigid way in which the First Amendment has often been applied. Has it not set up an absurd situation in which you can hardly say anything because somebody will be offended? That is basically the position the courts have taken with regard to explicitly religious expression. Ought it not be possible for local school districts, depending upon the composition of the local community, to work these things out in a spirit of good will, accommodating the people of the community? Might this not be better way of handling these problems than having rigid and doctrinaire decrees coming down from the Supreme Court?

The Intentless Constitution
of Justice William Brennan

Morton J. Frisch

Justice William J. Brennan, in a speech delivered at Georgetown University on October 12, 1985, said that when the justices interpret the Constitution, that interpretation must be undertaken with full consciousness that it is the community's interpretation that is sought. He does not posit fundamental constitutional principles as the standard, at least not initially. Rather he seeks the community's interpretation of the Constitution, by which he means the presently existing community or the present generation. It is apparent, however, that Brennan perceives a problem here, for he says that our commitment to self-governance in a representative democracy must somehow be reconciled with giving electorally unaccountable justices the power to invalidate the expressed desires of representative bodies inconsistent with higher law. There seems to be a recognition on his part that higher law (referring to fundamental constitutional principles) is not merely something distinct from the community's interpretation of the Constitution through its representatives, but something that the justices must or should take into account as part of their judicial function. Brennan is concerned with the matter of how to read the Constitution, that is, whether the Constitution presents a working paper for changing perspectives on government or whether it is properly seen as an embodiment of certain fundamental principles, the meaning of which can continue to be discerned even in the face of constant change.

Brennan then turns his attention to those who find legitimacy in fidelity to what they call "the intentions of the Framers" of the Constitution. He finds the most doctrinaire incarnation of this view in the requirement that justices discern exactly what the Framers thought about a question under consideration by the court and simply follow that intention in resolving the case before them. He questions the possibility of accurately gauging the intent of the Framers on matters concerning the application of principle to contemporary questions. He even goes so far as to question whether the idea of an original intention is a coherent way of thinking about a jointly drafted document meant to accommodate many positions and placate various interests. In other words, Brennan questions the very concept of the intentions of the Framers insofar as constitutional interpretation is concerned. He seems to be unaware of the fact that the American Constitution, despite its compromises and accommodations, was a contrivance of reason, a condensed, systematic, and abstract document with a coherence of its own. To deny the idea of an original intention is to deny that there was a thrust to the American Constitution, a thrust that was informed by principles and that gave the Constitution its distinctive character. The republicanism that characterizes the American Constitution represented a radical departure from the traditional republicanism of the Articles of Confederation in that it rested on separation of powers with a view to independent energetic executive power.

Brennan argues that those who would restrict claims of constitutional right to "the values of 1789 specifically articulated in the Constitution" abstain from adaptation of "overarching principles" to changes of social circumstances. In one and the same sentence he suggests that the values of 1789 articulated in the Constitution may be outmoded while he remains committed to overarching principles. Brennan posits, at least provisionally, a view that leaves substantive value choices to the majoritarian process, which he regards as a "more sophisticated" view than "the jurisprudence of original intent," but he concludes that it "ultimately will not do." He is apparently unwilling to abide by absolute majority rule, stating that it is the very purpose of a constitution "to declare certain values transcendent, beyond the reach of temporary political majorities." He confesses that one cannot read the constitutional text without admitting that it involves "substantive value choices," and therewith he places certain values beyond the power of any majority. Brennan admits, in other words, that a reasonable approach to interpreting the constitutional text must account for the existence of substantive value choices, but at the same time he accepts the uncertainty inherent in the effort to apply these transcendent values to present-day circumstances.

The problem for Brennan in the matter of constitutional interpretation is the tension between accounting for the existence of transcendent values on the one hand and applying these transcendent values to present-day circumstances on the other, since constitutional principles (or what he calls transcendent values) are hardly principles at all if they have no applicability to controversies arising in courts of law. The Constitution is a standard whether the judges like it or not. It is in this sense that Brennan says that transcendent values must be accounted for. Nevertheless, applying them to present-day circumstances, from Brennan's frame of reference, becomes a problem since the Framers did not address themselves, as he says, to specific, contemporary issues. His solution is that the justices must read the Constitution the only way they can, and that means determining what the words of the text mean in our time. It is unclear what this statement, on its face, means, but given the drift of his argument, it appears that the standard comes from perceived needs or prevailing values and not from the Constitution itself. This becomes clear from the following remark of his: "Our Constitution was not intended to preserve a preexisting society but to make a new one, to put in place new principles that the prior political community had not sufficiently recognized."

But Brennan might argue that those justices who claim to simply follow the intention of the Framers in resolving cases brought before them are too rigid, and that contemporary questions that the Founding Fathers had not anticipated must be dealt with on their own merits rather than torturing the constitutional text in order to find a solution. That argument would seem reasonable as long as dealing with cases and controversies not anticipated by the Framers on their own merits would mean making determinations on the basis of broad constructionism consistent with the intent of the Framers. But Brennan is locked into his stated position that the intent of the Framers on application of principle to specific, contemporary problems cannot be gauged accurately from our vantage point, and that it is far from clear whether the very idea of original intention is a coherent way of thinking about the Constitution. The question then becomes, How can we think about the Constitution? Brennan's view, at least in theory, is that the community's interpretation should be sought by the justices, an interpretation that almost always reflects current needs. But he backs off from this view at some point or other, if the community's views veer away from what is perceived by the justices to be the essential meaning of the Constitution. No matter how hard he tries, he cannot completely abandon the very notion he criticizes, the notion of substantive constitutional principles. Be that as it may, the Brennan statement on its face is highly problematic. It reduces the American Constitution to an artifact reflecting the values of 1789 and is unable to provide guidance for dealing with current problems and needs. It becomes clear that Brennan would replace the values of 1789, whenever he considered them outmoded, with his own values, which may or may not be consistent with the present community's values.

Brennan says that "judicial power [or the power of interpretation of the law] resides in the authority to give meaning to the Constitution"; but it is only fair to point out that he also says his burden of twenty-nine court terms has been "to draw meaning from the text." Of course he cannot mean both, and we know perfectly well which he does mean. It should be evident that interpretation of the law does not mean to "give" meaning to the law, but rather (in Hamilton's words) to "ascertain" its meaning, whether Brennan is aware of the difference or not. (See *Federalist* 78.) To give meaning to the Constitution would mean to revise the Constitution, but the judges do not have that power. The judges, as the guardians of the Constitution, are governed by the Constitution and thus constrained to look to the Constitution as a source of direction or enlightenment rather than the other way around. The Constitution is not simply a document elaborated by constitutional interpretation, as Brennan suggests, for the judges can be mistaken in their interpretation of the Constitution. He overestimates the interpretive role of the courts with respect to the Constitution.

Henry Steele Commager, the dean of American historians, supports the Brennan interpretation of the Constitution, emphasizing its flexibility and adaptability, something no one could reasonably deny. But what Commager means by flexibility becomes nakedly apparent when he says that Lincoln understood the Constitution to be flexible enough to enable him to do whatever was necessary to save the Union (*New York Times*, November 25, 1985, p. 31). Unfortunately Lincoln undermined whatever arguments he made for a flexible or broad interpretation of the Constitution by indicating that it might be necessary to suspend part of the Constitution in order to preserve the whole Constitution. In other words, Lincoln's suggestion that it might be necessary under certain circumstances to go outside the limits set by the Constitution indicates that it is not as flexible as Commager believes it to be, or as he thought Lincoln understood it to be. The fact is that the Constitution by definition has definite parameters that mark the limits of governmental authority. The Constitution, for example, does not sanction executive prerogative, except possibly for pardons and vetoes, and no matter how broadly executive power over foreign affairs may be construed, the executive has no authority to operate beyond and therefore in violation of the Constitution. Commager's notion of an endlessly flexible and adaptable Constitution would allow the judges to revise it on the basis of value judgments unsupported by the Constitution or the purposes of its Framers.

Brennan has no compunction in saying that the justices have the last word on the meaning of the Constitution; but, if we take his opening remarks seriously, it is a last word that reflects, in a very real sense, the community's interpretation. He later qualifies this position, however, by saying that the majoritarian process cannot resolve all matters of substantive policy and, by implication, that the justices are not always bound by the community's interpretation. Brennan says that when a justice perceives that an interpretation of the text (presumably the community's interpretation) has radically departed from the "essential meaning" of the text (presumably better understood by the justices than by the community), the justice is bound by a higher constitutional duty to expose the departure and point toward a different path. Not only does he reverse himself on the question of whether one can determine the essential meaning of the constitutional text, but he also argues that policies and programs not consistent with the transcendent values inherent in the constitutional text need to be reversed. In other words, Brennan inadvertently succumbs to the position from which he seeks to liberate himself.

Brennan maintains that constitutional clauses cannot be understood in terms of the intent of the Framers or the original understanding of the clause since we have no way of recovering the intent of the Framers, and furthermore, even if recoverable, their intentions are irrelevant to our contemporary problems and concerns. He even goes so far as to suggest that "each generation has the choice to overrule or add to the fundamental principles enunciated by the Framers," a principle reminiscent of the Jeffersonian idea of the sovereignty of the present generation. Brennan seeks liberation from the dead hand of the past. He sees the Constitution as a "living" or evolving document free of inherent meaning, a document, as it were, not rising above the assumptions of its age. It is important that the difference between Brennan and John Marshall, the founder of our constitutional law, be clearly understood. Marshall undertook the task of preserving fundamental constitutional principles while elaborating them so as to make them applicable to changing conditions. For him, the important objects and great outlines of the Constitution were permanent realities by which adjudication could and should be guided. But for Brennan, the abstract principles contained in the Constitution cannot provide substantial guidance in the formation of a reasoned opinion and therefore cannot be binding on the present generation.

Brennan says that "the genius of the Constitution rests . . . in the adaptability of its great principles to cope with current problems and current needs," but he previously said that "it is arrogant to pretend that from our vantage we can gauge accurately the intent of the Framers on application of principle to specific, contemporary questions." By adaptability of its great principles, he obviously means the interpretation or reinterpretation of its great principles, but he sees no arrogance in that. Interpretation, he explains, "must account for the transformative purpose of the text," that is, what the words of the text mean in our time. Brennan acknowledges the Constitution as a statement of broad principles, but of what value is the recognition of broad principles when you do not have meaning or intent to rest upon? He comes close to suggesting that there is no such entity as the American Constitution where norms are, in principle, discoverable.

Brennan believes that there cannot be any genuine knowledge of the specific intentions of the Framers or the original understanding of constitutional clauses. He expresses indignation against those who search for a single state of mind, something like a coherent intention. There is no reason to quarrel with the view that the Framers could not anticipate every problem to arise under the Constitution. They were not so shortsighted as to be unable to see that very many things must necessarily be left unfinished—the responsibility of future law-givers to work out—but an unfinished constitution is not an end-lessly flexible and adaptable constitution. Brennan attaches great importance to the work of constitutional interpretation, but that attachment is at bottom an attachment to the transformation of the Constitution without any authoritative guidance at all.

Brennan's fundamental position is unambiguously stated by Gordon Wood in his essay on "Democracy and the Constitution," where he argues that "there was not in 1787 a single 'true' or 'correct' interpretation of the Constitution," and furthermore that "the 'true' meaning, the 'true reality' of the Constitution will never be finally discovered," because it does not exist (How Democratic Is the Constitution?, ed. by R. Goldwin and W. Schambra, Washington, D.C., 1980, p. 4n). It may be inferred from this point of view (that is, that the Constitution has no correct interpretation) that there is no text, but only interpretation. The doctrine of the living Constitution is characterized by this view that the Constitution is changeable in its essence. One could say that the term *interpretation* as used by Brennan (to "give" rather than to "ascertain" meaning) serves no other purpose than to obscure his own predilections.

Brennan wants to make clear the correct way of interpreting the Constitution. But his argument does not succeed in clarifying for us whether the Constitution should simply be treated as a structuring text whose principles are subject to constant revision, or as a document containing an essential meaning whose revision is beyond the reach of temporary political majorities and courts of law. He has occasional glimpses of the possibility that the Constitution is an architectonic document, but he fails to appreciate or come to terms with that realization.

Interpreting the Constitution

Frederick Schauer

It is clear from almost everything that has been said about the Constitution throughout the course of this bicentennial year that what people are thinking about and talking about is the Constitution as it relates to the job that the Supreme Court has to do and how well it does it. But there is a side to the Constitution and to constitutional law that does not have a whole lot to do with the Supreme Court, and we ought to think about that Constitution before we embark on discussions and debates about what the Supreme Court ought to do.

I take it as a given that Ronald Reagan is not going to run for a third term. I also take it as a given that no twenty-seven-year-old is seriously going to consider running for the United States Senate, nor that any thirty-two-year-old will seriously consider running for the presidency of the United States, nor that bills voted on in the affirmative by only 42 percent of the voting members of Congress will be considered law. When we think about the Constitution, we ought to think about it primarily as a document that gives instructions to public officials and to the citizenry; as a document whose instructions, by and large, are followed; whose instructions, by and large, are not linguistically problematic; and as a document whose instructions frequently present clear mandates based on language not requiring interpretation by the courts. Courts, and for that matter lawyers as well, are professional nibblers around the edges. They are professionally preoccupied with the slice of legal life that calls into question the language of a law or a constitution in cases in which its normally clear meaning becomes unclear.

To generalize from what courts do or from what lawyers do to what the law is all about is somewhat like asking a pathologist about the human body. Ultimately, lawyers and judges are concerned with the pathological edge of the law—the areas in which the normally or frequently clear mandates of law fail us, whether intentionally or accidentally. We are correct to think that courts are important, and we are correct to think that the Supreme Court is more important than other courts, but we are mistaken to think that law is all about what courts do, and we are mistaken to think that constitutional law is all about what the Supreme Court does.

Some of you may remember that some years back President Ronald Reagan had an operation requiring that he be under general anesthetic. He consulted with his advisers about what to do in the light of the appropriate constitutional provisions dealing with presidential disability. His advisers gave him some advice I think was wrong. Other people suggested that the president ought to have done things differently from the way he did in terms of the actual temporary transfer of power to the vice president. But the important thing about this issue is that it was even an issue. There has never been a case about presidential disability in the Supreme Court. Given a number of doctrines about the kinds of things the Supreme Court will and will not hear, I can assure you with some confidence that there never will be. Nevertheless, despite the noninvolvement of the courts it was a constitutional issue thought about seriously by political officers.

Of somewhat more immediate interest, some of you may remember that the precursor of the Indianapolis Anti-Pornography Ordinance was a similar ordinance in Minneapolis. And some of you may be aware of the fact that the reason there was no court test of the Minneapolis ordinance is that the mayor of Minneapolis vetoed the ordinance—not because he thought it was a bad idea, but because he thought it was unconstitutional. He is not the Supreme Court. Still, he took it upon himself, as all public officials ought to do, to take his oath of office seriously, to uphold the Constitution, and to think about the fact that the Constitution speaks to all of us. Very often, whether it be when the mayor of Minneapolis vetoes an ordinance or when Ronald Reagan decides not to run for a third term, these issues take place not even in the shadow of but outside of the kinds of issues that the Supreme Court is normally concerned with.

Having said that, however, I do not want to deny completely the importance and central position in American life of the Supreme Court of the United States. As we think about the Constitution 184 years after *Marbury* v. *Madison*, the Supreme Court is undoubtedly a major player. One of the reasons is that not all of the clauses of the Constitution are quite as clear as that in the Twenty-second Amendment limiting the president to two terms in office. Others are quite indeterminate: "Congress shall make no law abridging the freedom of speech," according to the First Amendment; the Fourteenth Amendment adds, "nor shall any State deny to any person the equal protection of the laws nor deprive any person of life, liberty, or property without due process of law"; the Eighth Amendment contains a prohibition of "cruel and unusual punishment"; the Fourth Amendment prohibits "unreasonable searches and seizures"; and so on. What are we to do to interpret the Constitution where it is this vague? What does the Constitution say when it speaks in such imprecise language? As I have suggested, that is an issue for all of us. But let me for a moment focus somewhat more closely on what the Constitution might say to the Supreme Court, and how the Supreme Court should interpret what the Constitution says when it is dealing with clauses of this degree of indeterminacy.

As will become apparent, my views on these issues are somewhat different from Dr. Frisch's. Still, I do not wish to describe them only in those terms. Although Justice Brennan and I have never spoken about the issue, I think it is fair to say that we have an agreement that I will not speak for him and he will not speak for me. Nevertheless, there is likely to be some affinity between what I say and the views of Justice Brennan as described by Dr. Frisch. Yet there are different ways of characterizing the issues, and I would like to explore some of them.

We have in the Constitution such open-ended language as "equal protection of the laws," "due process of law," "cruel and unusual punishment," "the freedom of speech," and so on. What are we to do with those particularly indeterminate clauses when we are faced with real cases, real decisions to make, and real world choices in our lives and in judges' lives as they approach the cases before them? One common answer, indeed one that we just heard discussed and defended, is that we should look in some form to the original intentions of a certain specified group of people, whether they be characterized in terms of Framers, Ratifiers, or whatever. I do not want to deal particularly with the issues of how we can tell what the intention was and whose intention matters. I agree that we can know about original intention with tolerable accuracy. But the fact that we can tell does not make it relevant. The fact that I know what the Mayflower Compact says does not make the Mayflower Compact a privileged source of constitutional interpretation. I agree that although there are historiographical problems, frequently we can have a good idea of what original intent tells us; yet that does not give it any particular authority. The question we have to ask is, Why would those intentions have some authority?

We ought to start with the assumption—and it is clear to me that this is where Dr. Frisch and I have our major disagreements— that there is nothing in the nature of language that makes the meaning of language synonymous with the intentions of the people who use that language. Let us conduct a little experiment. You go into an antique shop. There, in the antique shop, is a daily newspaper from New South Wales, Australia, April 28, 1847. You pick it up.

Can you read it? Probably a fair amount of it, despite the fact that you know nothing about the author of that newspaper, and that you share little culturally in common other than the common heritage of something that we call the English language. Your understanding is not perfect. Cultural differences stand between us and the Australia of 1847. Nevertheless, you can get a moderately good idea of what that newspaper is saying because of a remarkable feature of language, linguistic autonomy. What is remarkable about language is that words carry meaning that we can identify without probing into the brains of the people who are using those words. That is how we are able to communicate everyday. If the shells wash up on the beach in a configuration that looks like C-A-T, we are likely immediately to think of small, furry house pets, rather than zebras, and that is because symbols themselves, by convention, can suggest meaning.

So we ought to start from the assumption that language-meaning and speaker-meaning are not synonymous. They are different, and the fact that we may want to be faithful to a written constitution as best we can does not suggest that we must necessarily go back to original intent.

If nothing in the nature of language mandates use of original intent, then it appears as well that there is nothing in the nature of law that requires recourse to original intent. Think about the task that many of us face late in the evening on April 15 of every year. We pick up and read and try to understand and interpret a rather lengthy series of instructions about our income taxes. And for our purposes, that is the law. And what the law is for us is what words on a piece of paper reasonably mean, what they mean according to the conventions of the language. Hence, we can imagine having law without taking original intent to be central. We do not think about the intentions of Congress when we read our tax instructions; we assume that those intentions are embodied in the instructions, in the statutes, in the regulations that we read. There is something very special about law that suggests that it is the very putting down of words on the piece of paper, and fixing those words over time, that defines the enterprise and defines the practice.

I have just, therefore, described the other side of a dispute that pervades every one of the interpretive disciplines. The dispute between intentionalism and nonintentionalism exists in almost every field involving interpretation. Think about art, for example. I go to a museum and I see on the walls a painting, and the inscription below the painting says *Guernica*, by Pablo Picasso. Assume I know nothing about the painting. I look at the painting, I see what looks like fear and horror, and I say the painting is about fear and horror. Then I comment that it is about, say, the fear and horror that people feel when they live in a dangerous, inner-city, urban environment. Suppose the person next to me, knowing somewhat more about art, says, "Oh no, that's not right. It's about the Spanish Civil War." Is that a conclusive, knock-down answer or not? What I want to suggest is that although my answer is no, and others might answer yes, there is a serious dispute within the philosophy of art as to which we can and should argue. Does the painter or the poet or the playwright have any pride of place as an interpreter once he or she sends forth a creation to the public? Or is it in the nature of the painting and writing and constitution writing and lawmaking that one is committed to the meaning of the words one uses regardless of what one intends? Is one committed to the conventions surrounding the symbols, whether they be artistic or linguistic, regardless of what one intends? Consider the law of defamation. If, in public, I accuse someone of being a child molester who is not, in fact, a child molester, and I then say, "Well, to me a child molester is just someone who really enjoys playing with children a great deal to the exclusion of his professional life." The courts will quite properly answer, "Tough. That's not what *child molester* means, given the linguistic conventions of this community. And you, by being a member of this community and speaking this language, are committed to the meaning of the terms you use."

So let us return to the open-ended terms of the Constitution. Let us return to free speech, to equal protection, to due process, to cruel and unusual punishment, and so on. One can and should say that the Constitution writer using those terms is committed to their indeterminacy—committed to the fact that these are terms that look different from "thirty years of age." And these terms looked different to James Madison and his colleagues as well. James Madison was no dummy. Neither were the other people in Philadelphia. Many of them were lawyers—not fancy constitutional lawyers teaching in universities, but real lawyers. They wrote wills; they wrote deeds; they knew about precise language; they knew how to use precise language when they wanted to; and therefore, they knew what general language meant. And even if they did not, having used it, they were committed to it. They wrote for a country that was committed to it. To rewrite the general terms of the Constitution, to make the general terms into specific terms, is to rewrite the Constitution. And that, in effect, is what people like the attorney general of the United States want to do. They are the rewriters of the Constitution. They are the ones who are uncomfortable with the intentional or otherwise apparent indeterminacy of the document as it is in fact written. They are the ones who want to rewrite it. They are the ones who want to make the general terms specific. Why? Probably because they are interested in constraint for constraint's sake. That is not necessarily a bad goal. Strong arguments can be made that in the vehicle of state, the Constitution serves in some important sense as "the brakes," while the majoritarian bodies are the accelerators.

We could therefore have written a Constitution that made its constraints much more specific, to both interpreters and legislators. That might have been a good idea. But that is not the Constitution we, in fact, have. A good part of the Constitution we happen to have, be it perhaps mainly by historical accident, is not very specific. Much of it is indeed quite general. And we ought to think about whether it is appropriate to rewrite the general Constitution just because we are uncomfortable with some of the results that some of its authoritative interpreters have reached. Ultimately what I am saying is that we ought to think of the Constitution, at least the general clauses of the Constitution, as a frame without a picture. The clauses need some filling in. And what I have argued is that there is no natural or logical reason to assume from the nature of language or of law or of constitutions that that filling-in must necessarily come from original intent.

The courts, when they interpret in hard cases, are the painters on the canvas that exists within this frame. When I talk in terms of a frame, I suggest that there *are* limits. The suggestion that judges who interpret the Constitution according to contemporary values, or their own values, are violating the Constitution confuses the issue of whether they are going against what the words say—which I would not have them do ever—with whether they are adding content within the area of discretion linguistically permitted by the nature of the general language in the Constitution. And if they are filling-in without going beyond the constraints of the frame around this blank canvas, there is nothing in the nature of language or of law or of constitutionalism that suggests that it is illegitimate. We might want to rewrite our Constitution to make its words more specific, but we have not done that.

Now, what, within the frame, should judges do if in fact they are not going to engage in the historical exercise of looking for original intent? Ultimately what they are going to do—and few people who think seriously about the Constitution would deny this—is to some significant extent to make social, moral, and political choices substantially, if not completely, influenced by their own social, moral, and political outlooks.

I want to say just a couple of words about that before I finish. But first, let me at least note the important constraint of precedent. Courts operate on the assumption that what they did before has some weight because they did it before—not because it is right. The prior has priority because it is prior. That is not always the most intelligent way of making decisions. Nevertheless, it is part of the way courts make decisions, because courts are frequently assumed to be agents of stability for stability's sake. Therefore, courts do operate and ought to operate on the assumption that the interpretations that have put some flesh on the skeleton of the constitutional text are entitled to substantial deference by subsequent interpreters even if they disagree with the earlier decisions.

A conscientious Chief Justice Rehnquist, therefore, should at least give some deference to the decision of the Supreme Court in *Roe* v. *Wade*, the abortion case with which he disagreed, precisely because it has already been decided. At times, the justices actually do this. The Supreme Court for some years has been fighting about the issue of how to interpret Titles VI and VII of the Civil Rights Act of 1964 in terms of whether those statutes prohibit affirmative action or prohibit taking race into account in order to compensate for past discrimination. In previous decisions, Justices O'Connor and Stevens have been of the view that Titles VI and VII as they are written prohibit all use of race regardless of the purpose for which race is being used. They were in the minority in that opinion. In *Johnson* v. *Santa Clara County Transportation Agency* (55 U.S.L.W. 4379 [1987]), they said, in effect, that we fought what we thought was the good fight but we lost. We will now go along with the majority's interpretation even though we think it is wrong, and we will assume that that is the law. So precedent is part of the process that substantially narrows the size of the frame. Still, it is inevitable that judges will be making moral, political, and social decisions according to their own values.

To the extent that that is denied in public discourse, it is quite simply wrong—it happens and we all know it. This fact ought to tell us something about the process of appointing judges, but it also ought to say something about the process of giving advice and consent in the appointment process. Judges, if they are good lawyers, will recognize that their discretion to interpret is substantially constrained by text and precedents. But such judges will also recognize that when the constraints of text and precedents are behind them, when they are dealing with a case in which the constraints of text and precedent do not give them an answer, they are on their own and they are no longer lawyers. At that point, they are political figures, and above all, they are people. When we are thinking about interpretation, we have to think about interpreters; and when we are thinking about interpreters, we have to think of who the interpreters are. To avoid the inevitable personal, political, and social issues in the interpretive process is to be unrealistic. But to assume that it is all politics is to be equally unrealistic. Ultimately, contemporary debates are about who, which particular people, we want to constrain and why. I have a hunch that the debates may look different in ten years; they look different now from the way they looked ten years ago. These debates change depending on the nature of the issues before us. I am not sure that we can ever think about such debates outside the nature of the issues before us, but I have tried to suggest some possible ways of thinking about interpretation apart from the immediacy of the political issues on the agenda for today.

Some Reflections
on the Constitution
After Two Hundred Years

Richard B. Morris

This seems to me to be an appropriate time to reexamine three disparate but still timely aspects of our Constitution: the durable quality of that great charter; an explanation of why a consensus was so quickly achieved at Philadelphia; and the perpetual and insistent question: What is the Constitution and who finally decides what it says?

Curiously, whether by intention or accident, the Constitution did not declare itself to be *perpetual*, unlike the weak "perpetual" union—the Articles of Confederation that it succeeded. Even the historic Northwest Ordinance, adopted by Congress sitting in New York at the height of the sessions of the Constitutional Convention in Philadelphia, described that blueprint for the governance of the Northwest as a "perpetual" compact. Somehow that adjective was overlooked in the federal Constitution, along with the noun "compact."

True, in Gouverneur Morris's incomparable language, the Preamble declares its purposes "to form a more perfect Union" and "secure the blessings of liberty to ourselves and our posterity." President Washington in his farewell address speaks of "the efficacy and permanency of your Union." Still, that union, made "more perfect" by the Constitution, was nevertheless in later times said to be dissoluble at the pleasure of any state that might desire to secede. To put the question beyond controversy required a four-year Civil War and a Supreme Court decision. The North's military victory destroyed the doctrine that the Constitution was a compact of sovereign states, each with the right to secede from the Union. The Supreme Court confirmed this military decision in *Texas* v. *White* in 1869 when it declared, "The Constitution, in all its provisions, looks to an indestructible Union, composed of indestructible States."

One of the clues to the mystery of the durable nature of the Constitution is its plastic quality, making it applicable to a rapidly changing society. It was the deliberate intention of the Committee of Detail and its draftsman, Edmund Randolph, "to insert essential principles only" in order, to use his own words, to accommodate the Constitution "to times and events," and "to use simple and precise language and general propositions." Randolph's notion of confining a constitution to broad principles rather than cluttering up the document with unnecessary details was a master stroke that contributed much to that document's enduring suitability and relevance, and James Wilson of Pennsylvania contributed further to putting the Randolph draft into even smoother prose. Finally, the same principle of using precise language and general propositions was prudently followed by the Committee of Style, which under the swift and sure guidance of Gouverneur Morris and his talented colleagues gave us the final draft, a masterpiece of conciseness.

How different indeed from modern state constitutions, often extremely long, cluttered with minute details under which the general principles lie buried, often inspired by local and temporary needs. The great charter, a few parchment pages adopted in eighty-four working days, sticks to broad principles and has a dateless character lacking in so many of the bulky state constitutions that are closer to compiled statutes than to broad blueprints of governance.

A second observation about the Constitution helps explain its relatively speedy adoption and ability to secure ratification. When on the fiftieth anniversary of the establishment of the national government former President John Quincy Adams spoke of the federal Constitution as having been "extorted" from "the grinding necessity of a reluctant nation," he was attesting to the fact that only with a combination of bold innovations, compromise, and concession was it possible to frame and ratify the Constitution.

School texts invariably refer to the Great Compromise by which the small states were given equality in the Senate whereas the House of Representatives was made proportional to population. But even that compromise, credited to the delegates from Connecticut, included additional compromises. Once it was settled that the House was to be elected by the people, the issue arose whether the Senate was to be elected in the manner that democratic nationalist James Wilson proposed; by the House, in the plan Edmund Randolph sponsored; or by the state legislatures, an idea put forth by John Dickinson, the prestigious delegate from Delaware. The last suggestion was the one adopted, and it was a tribute to the delegates' concern about creating a federal rather than a national Constitution. However, in this case Wilson's vision proved the sharpest, as the Senate later came to be perceived as a tool of the big business interests that dominated the state legislatures. The Seventeenth Amendment, ratified in 1913, providing for direct election of senators by the people, vindicated James Wilson's judgment on this issue.

The large states had come out the victors in winning proportional representation in the House, but the Northern states could hardly permit the South to count black people (who were not eligible to vote) for purposes of representation and direct taxation. The result: another compromise by which representation and direct taxes in the lower House would be based on the white inhabitants, including white bound servants (a favored labor source in tobacco states like Maryland and Virginia), and three-fifths of all other persons, "except Indians not paying taxes." As a result a black person was counted as three-fifths of a white person, and virtually all Indians were excluded.

If the Great Compromise was a resolution of differences between the large and small states in their conception of the Union to be formed, the second major compromise came as a result of a confrontation between the North and the South. Now, everyone had agreed that giving the national government power over commerce was, along with the power to tax, a prime motive for calling the conventions first in Annapolis and later in Philadelphia. The Southern states had some second thoughts, however. States that exported farm staples to a world market felt that this clause would work to the advantage of the North, heavily engrossed in trade and shipping, while adding disproportionate costs to Southern exporters. To protect itself against possible discrimination, the South sought to require that commercial legislation have a two-thirds vote in each house to be enacted. James Madison, rising above sectional prejudices, prevailed upon the Convention to give Congress the power to regulate commerce by a simple majority vote.

Nonetheless, every regional concession brought its price and begot a compromise. Thus the slavery issue, which hitherto had been swept under the rug, came to the fore when the delegates took up the matter of levying import and export duties. The South proposed that Congress be forbidden to prohibit the importation of slaves, or to levy taxes on such importation, as well as trading of slaves between states. Over the surprised objections of George Mason, Virginia's greatest libertarian, and a divided North, a compromise was worked out whereby no prohibition of the importation of slaves could be permitted before the year 1808. Even the North divided on this crucial vote; nor was there a solid South: Virginia voted "nay." Thus was slavery acknowledged, though not by name, in the Constitution and in two other compromises—the three-fifths rule for representation in the House of Representatives and direct taxes and the provision for the return to their owners of fugitive "persons held to service or labour," a description used to avoid the word *slaves.*

Still the Philadelphia delegates continued to compromise. The proposal for a strong presidency advanced in the Virginia Plan and one of the distinctive features of our Constitution resulted in a bundle of compromises. First, it was decided that the chief executive was to be a single person, not a committee or plural executive as had been originally, if vaguely, proposed. He would serve for four years (other proposals had ranged from a life term to a single seven-year term) and he was to be eligible for reelection. He would have a qualified veto (one that could be overridden by the legislative branch), not an absolute veto as Madison had urged. He would not be chosen by Congress, as the Virginia Plan had proposed, nor selected directly by the people, as James Wilson and Gouverneur Morris would have preferred. Instead, the final decision, after countless proposals, was to have the president elected by electors who would be chosen in each state "in such manner" as its legislators might "direct." This plan, perhaps conceived to propitiate the states, proved instead a victory for both nationalism and democracy, for very shortly after 1789 *all* the state legislatures provided for the election of their states' presidential electors by popular vote. If no candidate had a majority of the electoral vote, the ultimate choice would be made from the five highest candidates by the House of Representatives. However, in choosing the president the House would vote by states, each state having one vote. Thus, the electoral college proved to be a compromise whereby the people indirectly, rather than the state legislatures, would make the choice, and if no candidate had a majority vote, the House, then dominated by a combination of Southern and small states, would be in a controlling position to decide the election.

Perhaps the ablest defense of these compromises and concessions came from *The Federalist*, where Madison, while conceding that the Constitution was not a "faultless" document, admitted that the convention's delegates "were either satisfactorily accommodated by the final act; or were induced to accede to it out of a deep conviction of the *necessity of sacrificing private opinions* and *partial interests* to the *public good*, and by a despair of seeing this necessity diminished by the delays or by new experiments" (*Federalist* 37).

Finally, and certainly most important in terms of the safeguards for the people, the chief criticism leveled against the Constitution when it was finally submitted to the people for ratification was the failure to incorporate a bill of rights. In ratifying the Constitution a number of states included bills of rights among their recommendatory amendments. To ensure such compliance New York even urged that a second convention be called. The prospect of a second convention, which might very well undo the great work that had been accomplished in Philadelphia, horrified James Madison. Once elected to the House of Representatives, the Virginian reduced more than two hundred proposed amendments to twelve, of which ten were ratified. The Bill of Rights, as the first ten amendments are called, although deemed unnecessary by the leading nationalists and the authors of *The Federalist*, proved to be the great concession to quiet fears the public nurtured about the intention of the new government toward guaranteeing civil liberties. This concession was Madison's noblest bequest to the nation.

Thus, by compromise and concession a framework of a federal government was hammered out and the bicentennial attests to its lasting contribution and present relevance to that "more perfect Union" to which the Framers were committed.

If there was controversy from the very start about the scope and intent of the Constitution, that controversy has continued to the present day—in fact, it has heated up over the insistence of a contemporary attorney general that the *court in interpreting the Constitution is bound by the intent of the Framers*. This question, debated in many quarters during the bicentennial of the Constitution, addresses itself to the public's conception of the Constitution: is it a charter carved in stone or a document adjustable by interpretation to rapidly changing social, economic, and technological demands, along with moral values? If the Constitution looks "forward to remote futurity," as Hamilton described it in the *The Federalist*, how flexible did he consider the Constitution to be?

Are the courts bound by the debates at the convention and the state ratifying conventions or are the courts bound by the "express words" of the Constitution? And if the latter is true, are they bound by the meaning of those words in 1787 or in the 1980s? Certainly the meaning that the drafters wished to communicate may arguably differ from the meaning the reader is warranted in deriving from the text, and the two might not be identical.

What we do know, from studying the notes of debates on the framing of the Constitution, is that it was the Framers' primary expectation that the Constitution would be interpreted in accord with its *express language*. Terms proposed were criticized as "vague" or "indefinite," and there were debates then that continue to this day about how much scope was given the president and Congress in investing the latter with the power "to declare war."

Since the debates were secret and mostly not published until after James Madison's death some fifty years later, there is no indication that the Framers intended future interpreters to extract intention from reference to sources secret and unavailable. Nevertheless, in the debates over ratification, worries were expressed by the Antifederalists that broad construction would be placed on the enumerated powers by Congress and federal judiciary. At the New York ratification convention John Jay sought to allay these fears by insisting that the document involved "no sophistry, no construction, no false glosses, but simple inference from the obvious operation of things." And Madison in *The Federalist* was at pains to point out that improper construction of the Constitution could be remedied through amendment or by election "of more faithful representatives to annul the acts of the usurpers."

One of the most flagrant examples of determining the intent of the Framers is in the construction of the "necessary and proper" clause. Both Madison and Hamilton served on the Committee of Style that was responsible for the final wording of the Constitution. In *Federalist* 44 Madison argued for a liberal interpretation of the "necessary and proper" clause in a way that must have delighted Hamilton, who was later to take the same position in defending the creation of the first Bank of the United States—to the dismay of Madison. In fact, the convention had rejected a proposal to give Congress explicit power to charter corporations. Only after he became involved with Jefferson in the party assault on Hamilton's financial policies did Madison in effect repudiate his no. 44 and adopt the theory of "strict construction." Yet it was to be Hamilton's interpretation of the scope of the "necessary and proper" clause that President Washington accepted and that Chief Justice Marshall would later embrace. Indeed, Hamilton anticipated the later assumption by the Supreme Court of powers for the federal government on the basis of three clauses of the Constitution, which, in addition to the necessary and proper clause, included the general welfare clause and the commerce clause. Yet who would argue today that the general welfare clause as originally designed supported the more modern concept of a welfare state or, though some scholars would insist, that the commerce clause was intended to cover manufacturing and virtually all forms of economic activity?

In *Federalist* 37, Madison, then sharing Hamilton's views, argued that the "intent" of any legal document is the product of the interpretive process and not some fixed meaning that the author locks into the document's text at the outset. He ventured so far as to declare that even the meaning of God's Word "is considered dim and doubtful, by the cloudy medium through which it is communicated" when God condescends to address people in their own languages. It was up to the courts, Hamilton argued in a later *Federalist* letter, to fix the meaning and operation of laws, including the Constitution, and the courts could be expected to use the rules of common sense to determine the "natural and obvious sense" of the Constitution's provisions.

The question of the intention of the Philadelphia Framers came up in one of the first great controversial decisions handed down by the Supreme Court presided over by John Jay. *Chisholm* v. *Georgia* considered the question, Could a state be sued by a private citizen of another state? The language of the Constitution was, to say the least, ambiguous. In Article III the judicial power could extend to controversies "between a state and citizens of another state." In the debates on ratification the Framers went to great pains to deny that the Constitution would affect the states' sovereign immunity. Even Hamilton gave such assurances in *Federalist* 81. Yet a majority of the court, construing the wording of the text, held that the text was intended to allow suits against a state. The state did not think so, and few amendments overruling a Supreme Court decision were adopted more speedily than the Eleventh Amendment, which upheld the states' immunity to such actions.

Indubitably the Virginia and Kentucky resolutions written by Jefferson and Madison, aimed at the Alien and Sedition acts (but not adopted by any other state) and affirming the right of the state legislatures to pass on the validity of federal statutes, presented a vision of the United States as a league of sovereign states—closer to the original compact idea of the Articles of Confederation and closer to the Antifederalist position than that espoused by their opponents. The Federalists, on the contrary, had insisted that the Constitution was a grant of authority from the sovereign people, while preserving important federal elements. The Virginia and Kentucky resolutions, contrary to the historic facts about the making of the Constitution and the plain language of the Preamble, established themselves as political orthodoxy and stood virtually unchallenged until the nullification crisis of 1828–32.

Yet in his later years Madison insisted that "as a guide in expounding and applying the provisions of the Constitution, the debates and incidental decisions of the Convention can have no authoritative character."

What counted then, in Madison's eyes, were precedents derived from "authoritative, deliberate and continued decisions." Thus Madison, who had originally phrased the Bill of Rights, sought to bind the states as well as Congress—a phrasing that mysteriously disappeared from the final product, which speaks only of Congress and not the states. He would have rejoiced at the modern Supreme Court's interpretation of the Fourteenth Amendment as incorporating prohibitions upon the states as well as Congress in regard to most of the Bill of Rights.

Indeed, what has contributed to the durability and survival of the Constitution is its capacity to adapt to a changing nuclear space society utterly different from the horse-and-buggy age of the Founding Fathers. It has been remarked before, and it is worth repeating now, that shortly before the Constitutional Convention assembled in Philadelphia a mob put an alleged witch to death in that city. Just a few weeks later most of the delegates went down to the banks of the Delaware to see a demonstration of Fitch's steamboat—so utterly divided was the climate of knowledge at that time. Obscurantism still held out in pockets of prejudice, while science and technology were already preparing society for the great industrial and technological revolution that lay ahead. A first amendment setting up a wall of separation between church and state and guaranteeing freedom of religion was adopted by a people who were already facing one of the great fundamentalist religious revivals of our history.

The Constitution made provision for such adjustments, and in the course of time for providing the equality promised in the Declaration of Independence. It provided amendments that, among other things, ended slavery, and provided for equal justice for black and white, voting rights for women, direct election of senators, an end to the poll tax, and suffrage for eighteen-year-olds previously eligible for the military draft but not for the franchise.

But not by amendments alone has the Constitution been reshaped— actions of the three branches have broadened its text and applied its principles to specific situations only dimly perceived by the Framers. As early as the administration of President George Washington the principle of executive privilege was upheld, the rights of the president to dismiss appointees accepted, the Cabinet, not mentioned in the Constitution, created, the right of the president to declare neutrality without consulting the Senate established, and the House of Representatives' power to withhold appropriations for treaties it did not approve of in essence denied. Finally, a party system emerged, a system that none of the Founding Fathers anticipated, that Washington deplored in his Farewell Address, and that was considered a cause of faction and divisiveness. Yet, as we see it today, political parties are accepted as the touchstone of a democratic society, and the repression of opposition parties is considered one of the most viable symptoms of a republican state.

Yet despite these enlargements and glosses upon the Constitution made by both the president and Congress over the past two centuries, it is the high court that bears the brunt of criticism for charges of straying from the intent of the Framers and of practicing what amounts to judicial legislation to effect due process, equal justice, voting equality, and the rights of privacy even in areas where it is doubtful that a majority of the nation's citizens support such advanced positions.

Charges rang in the halls of the ratifying conventions back in 1787–88 and are re-echoed today that entrusting final interpretation of the Constitution to the courts insulates the judges from electoral responsibility. Federal judges can be removed only by impeachment, which is justifiable for misbehavior but not for deviating from prevailing political norms. No federal judge has ever been impeached and removed from the bench because his decisions defied popular opinion. The failure to remove Associate Justice Chase settled that issue long ago. Alexander Hamilton defended the court's special position as essential to the judiciary's independent role as guardian of the Constitution's limits on power. That, of course, is the very issue that provokes criticism of the federal judiciary today. The court is increasingly presented with cases that deal with social issues—school busing, prayer in schools, desegregation, affirmative action, abortion, privacy—and litigants insist that the judicial branch fill the vacuum created by the lack of direction on these subjects from the other two branches of government, which are subject to the electoral process.

True, some of these issues divide the country very sharply, perhaps even more sharply than the slavery issue divided the nation at the time of the Dred Scott decision, where an unaccountable and sharply divided court adopted a stance that triggered a civil war and remained to be countermanded by the amendments that came out of that tragic conflict.

No single branch of the government can evade the issue of accountability for interpreting the Constitution. The president fills vacancies on the court, usually picking persons who reflect his constitutional views. In requiring the president to swear to "preserve, protect, and defend the Constitution," the public expects him to determine if and when it is being threatened. Lincoln, in his first inaugural, looked neither to the courts nor to Congress to decide that this was an indissoluble union. He explicitly assumed that authority and took the full burden upon his own shoulders. "I hold," he declared, "that in contemplation of universal law, and of the Constitution, the Union of these States is perpetual."

And Congress, too, cannot escape responsibility, since, beginning with the Judiciary Act of 1789, it has set the parameters of the federal courts' jurisdiction, and, save for the jurisdiction outlined in Article II, Congress can enlarge or diminish the scope of litigation that is justifiable by the federal courts.

And finally, we the people have the power through the ballot box, albeit that power has seldom been used directly to affect the trend of judicial decisions. The most startling example is the election of 1936; six weeks after the election the Supreme Court in obvious response to public opinion began to yield to the president's and Congress's constitutional views. But that example is dramatic and virtually without parallel. Indeed, few citizens consciously or systematically use their ballots to register constitutional interpretations. This omission leaves officials to resolve most conflicts among themselves; but when senators, representatives, and presidents take actions on constitutional issues, they are subject to the potential of reprisals at the polls against themselves and their parties.

There is a provision in the Constitution for amendment by calling a convention, but the Framers—having themselves violated their instructions by overthrowing rather than revising the Articles of Confederation—were loath to see a second convention possibly undo their great work. And despite the number of states that have gone on record recently to call for such a second convention (ostensibly for a balanced budget amendment), the calls are varied and imprecise and the dangers to the durable structure of the nation seem too great to bear the risk.

In the long run the Constitution will continue to function as long as it responds to the needs of our country for the creation of a just society and adheres to the other objectives set forth in the Preamble: "to insure domestic tranquillity, provide for the common defense, promote the general welfare, and secure the blessings of liberty to ourselves and our posterity." For two hundred years the Constitution has kept those goals in our minds, despite perplexing issues and the constantly changing values of the American nation. No worthier goals can be set for the great charter as it moves into its third century.

Schedule of Events for
the Ball State University/Muncie Community
Celebration of the Bicentennial of the Constitution
and Northwest Ordinance of 1787

October 21, 1986

"The Constitution and the Northwest Ordinance: Governing a New Nation," Lecture by Dr. Andrew R. L. Cayton, Associate Professor of History, Ball State University

Forum Room, L. A. Pittenger Student Center

October 28, 1986

"American Decorative Arts: The Roccoco to the Neo-Classic," Lecture by Mr. Alain G. Joyaux, Director, Ball State University Art Gallery

Francis Brown Lounge, Ball State University Art Gallery

November 4, 1986

"Writing the Wrongs: American Literature in Defense of the New Nation," Lecture by Dr. Robert D. Habich, Associate Professor of English, Ball State University

Forum Room, L. A. Pittenger Student Center

November 11, 1986

"The World of Jefferson and Bulfinch: Neo-Classical Architecture for a New Republic," Lecture by Dr. J. A. Chewning, Assistant Professor of Architecture, Ball State University

Auditorium, College of Architecture and Planning

January 27, 1987

Town Meeting on the First Amendment to the Constitution and Freedom of Speech

First Presbyterian Church

February 22, 1987

" 'An Assembly of Demi-Gods': The Formation of the Constitution," a dramatic presentation on the Constitution, produced and directed by Dr. Judy E. Yordon, Professor of Theatre, Ball State University

Muncie Civic Theatre

98

March 25, 1987

Town Meeting on the First Amendment to the Constitution and Freedom of Religion

First Presbyterian Church

April 28, 1987

Town Meeting on Interpreting the Constitution

First Presbyterian Church

June 27, 1987

Bicentennial Concert-on-the-Green by the Muncie Symphony Orchestra, Leonard Atherton, Music Director

Arts Terrace, Ball State University

August 17 to October 2, 1987

"The Constitution, Legacy of Liberty," an exhibition of original documents related to the United States Constitution and the Northwest Ordinance of 1787

Special Collections, Bracken Library, Ball State University

September 16, 1987

"1787: Legacy of Liberty for Hoosiers," Lecture by Dr. James H. Madison, Editor of the *Indiana Magazine of History* and Associate Professor of History, Indiana University, Bloomington

Bracken Library, Ball State University

September 17, 1987

"James Madison," a dramatic interpretation by Dr. James Soles, Professor of Political Science at the University of Delaware

Pruis Hall, Ball State University

September 21, 1987

"Some Reflections on the Constitution after 200 Years," Lecture by Dr. Richard B. Morris, Gouverneur Morris Professor of History Emeritus, Columbia University

Forum Room, L. A. Pittenger Student Center

October 28, 1987

"The Living Constitution," Lecture by Dr. Michael Kammen, Newton C. Farr Professor of American History and Culture, Cornell University

Forum Room, L. A. Pittenger Student Center

sity

tion

Dr. Davi
Professor ——————————— l Science
Departm
Ball State

Mr. Doug ——————— Esq.
Executive ——————— y, Radcliff
Ball Brotl

Dr. Steph ——————— orporate
Professor
Departme
and Cri
Ball State ——————— nt, Chairman
——————— Science

Dr. Andre
Associate ——————— Ball Center
Ball State ——————— Community

Richard A
Judge
Delaware

Dr. R. Sheldon Duecker
Senior Minister
High Street United Methodist Church

Joseph Edwards, Esq.
Shirey & Edwards

Mr. Robert A. Holt
Vice President for Community
  and Government Relations
Ontario Corporation

Dr. Joseph A. Losco
Associate Professor of Political
  Science
Ball State University

Mr. Jack McNew
Administrative Assistant—Elementary
  Education
Muncie Community Schools

Editor
The Muncie Star

Mr. David Tambo
Head of Special Collections
Bracken Library
Ball State University

Dr. C. Warren Vander Hill
Provost and Vice President for
  Academic Affairs
Ball State University

Dr. Sally Jo Vasicko
Professor and Chairperson
Department of Political Science
Ball State University

Mrs. Sandra Worthen